Kent Crimes and Disasters

by

Bill Bishop

Geerings of Ashford Ltd.,
Ashford, Kent, England

Kent Crimes and Disasters

Geerings of Ashford Ltd.,
Ashford, Kent, England

First Published 1993

© Bill Bishop

All rights reserved. No part of this publication may be reproduced, stored in a retreival system or transmitted, in any form, or by any means, electronic, mechanical, photocopying, recording or otherwise, without the prior permission of the Copyright owners.

ISBN 1 873953 09 7

This book has been typeset in 10 on 11 point Times Roman and printed by Geerings of Ashford Ltd., Ashford, Kent, England.

Foreword

As a keen and dedicated Man of Kent, I have always taken and hopefully displayed, a keen interest in the County's history and studied it accordingly. During my researches, I came across, as I expected, many fascinating and absorbing stories relating to major disasters, crimes and the unforgiveable felony of murder. Murder is of course, a revolting and terribly cruel deed. Having said that, I have found that the majority of murder cases wallow in a morass of mystery and intrigue. To me this bestows on such crimes, a fluctuating degree of interest.

Since I left the Royal Marines in 1950 and joined the Kent Constabulary the very same day, I have written numerous articles, which form the title of this book and a few which do not slot into that category. Now, I have selected what I consider to be the most interesting, the most appealing and if you like, the most entertaining and included them in this book. One reason for this revolves around my surprising discovery that many of my peers, both male and female, knew virtually nothing of the events and crimes outlined in my manuscript. In the main. this is simply because most of my stories date back long before the inception of the ubiquitous television and the spotlight of publicity never focused on them.

Of course, I do not expect everyone to be infatuated with history in any of its guises, but we should all remind ourselves that whether we like it or not, we create history every minute, every hour and every day. The now legendary Henry Ford was wrong when all those years ago he pedantically announced to the world - "History is Bunk". Ironically and justifiably, that great idol of the world's car industry, now shares the same historical pedestal as many other American inventors and pioneers.

Right:
The destroyed Promenade and Westbrook Pavilion from 'When the sea took charge. The flooding of Margate, 1953', page 19

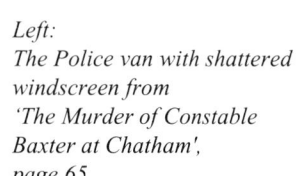

Left:
The Police van with shattered windscreen from 'The Murder of Constable Baxter at Chatham', page 65

Right:
American Armed Servicemen relax after a gun battle from 'The Manston Massacre, August 24th, 1955', page 87

Left:
Ashford Police Station. circa 1870, from 'A Bent Copper of the Last Century', page 75

Acknowledgements

I would like to express my gratitude to Mr. Robert Geering for his encouragement in this venture, and indeed, his confidence. I would also like to pay tribute to the hard-working members of his publishing staff, who were exceedingly helpful and very courteous.

Contents

Murder on the Marshes 7

The Execution of John Any Bird Bell, age 14. 13

When the sea took charge. The flooding of Margate, 1953 . . 19

The Great Fire of Wye, 1889 25

The Gestapo Chief of North Foreland 31

The Wrong Victim. (a very strange murder) 37

Rape and Murder on the Black Path 43

Murder in the Village School 49

The Murder of Caroline Trayler (a guilty man goes free). . . . 57

The Crimes and Punishments of Knatchbull, Meredith and Mann 61

The Murder of Constable Baxter at Chatham 65

The Death of the Battleship 'Bulwark' in 1914 69

A Bent Copper of the Last Century 75

Battle of the Dover Straits 81

The Manston Massacre, August 24th, 1955 87

A Foul Murder in Room 66 91

Murder on the Marshes

As a Police Constable serving in the historic and old naval town of Sheerness in 1954, Wednesday February 10th proved to be singularly memorable for me. Memorable, because, for the whole of the afternoon, I was instructed to sit in one of the old Victorian cells of Sheerness Police Station with a man who, 19 hours before, had coldbloodedly killed his prospective father-in-law. The victim was Herbert Victor Ketley, a 40-year-old motor mechanic, who lived at 31 Swale Road, Queenborough, a few miles from Sheerness. The murderer was James Reginald Doohan, a 24 year old labourer, who lived at Borough Road, Queenborough, a few minutes walk from the Ketley house, where Bert Ketley lived with his wife and his eighteen-year-old stepdaughter - Yvonne Deighton.

Now, Doohan and Yvonne had been walking out together for some three years and James Doohan was firmly convinced that Yvonne would eventually marry him. It was not to be; just a few weeks before the murder, which occurred on the evening of Tuesday 9th February, Yvonne informed Doohan that she was not at all sure that she loved him enough to take such an important step. At the enchanting age of eighteen, Yvonne was entitled to expect and get much more out of life than she would have done had she married James Doohan. Her decision had a shattering effect on Doohan and immediately, he concluded, quite wrongly as it happened, that Yvonne's stepfather had put the wedge in and turned her against him. He made this abundantly clear in his statement to the Police early on Wednesday morning.

When Doohan was serving in the Army in 1948, he was considered to be suffering from schizophrenia; and evidence to this effect was given at his trial. No doubt he was still suffering from some sort of mental disorder in 1954, for his belief that Ketley was responsible for Yvonne's rejection of his love soon became an obsession and then a positive certainty. It seems that on February 8th, when Yvonne again reiterated her statement to Doohan, he made up his mind that enough was enough and Ketley must die. Yvonne had told him that she wanted nothing to do with him in addition to her rejection of his advances and it is logical to assume that this was a severe blow to his ego and his pride. On the morning of 9th February, Doohan had decided on a cool, callous and calculating plan of murder. His first step was to borrow a shotgun and cartridges from one of his mates, on the pretext that he wished to do some shooting on the marsh. This was quite true of course, for at about 7 p.m. that night he called at Ketley's home and told him a convincing yarn that a man was injured on the marshes and Doohan needed the assistance of Ketley to get the man to the main road before calling an ambulance. When she gave evidence, Mrs Ketley stated that she saw her husband leave the house with Doohan and walk towards the marshes. It is doubtful whether Doohan entered the house, assuming he had the shotgun hidden under his coat; this explains why Mrs Ketley didn't see the weapon.

What happened when the two men reached the desolate wastes of Rushenden Marshes is best explained by Doohan in the statement he made to the C.I.D. at Sheerness Police Station at 3.15 a.m. on Wednesday. After the full caution had been administered and also written in full at the top of the statement form some six hours after Doohan's arrest, he said (this was dictated to a C.I.D. Officer). "I detested Yvonne's stepfather and I made up my mind to do him harm. I knew he was the cause of the trouble between Yvonne and me." He then described how he contrived to walk a few paces behind Ketley once they reached the marshes. "I put the barrel of the gun a few inches away from the back of his head and neck; I knew he wouldn't feel it there - I pulled the trigger and that was it. There must have been a lot of blood but as it was dark I didn't see much, as he lay on the ground I felt for his pulse but found none and none from his heart area. It was then I knew he was dead; I knew that my work was finished as far as he was concerned." Doohan was well aware that he had committed murder - a savage premediated killing, and this did not prevent him walking the mile or more to Queenborough Police Office on the main road leading from Queenborough. Having knocked on the blue-painted office door and rousing Police Sergeant Chatfield, he handed him the shotgun and said: "I've just killed a man, you'd better have this." Evidence of arrest was given by Detective Sergeant Jock Robertson, although I would have thought that Sergeant Chatfield would have made the arrest immediately Doohan told him what had happened. As it was, the Detective Sergeant went on to describe how at nine p.m. on that fateful night, Doohan led him and several other Police officers to the scene of the murder, a desolate spot well away from the main road and close to the banks of the River Swale. The medical evidence of the pathologist who carried out the post mortem examination, included the fact that the unfortunate Ketley had sustained a head wound caused by gunshot pellets. From past experience I would have expected that at least half of the head and neck had been blasted asunder.

Following Doohan's appearance before the Sittingbourne Magistrates on 10th February, the first of several before he was committed for trial, which was the usual procedure, I was detailed to sit with Doohan in his cell for the best part of three hours. Until, that is, he was conveyed to Canterbury Prison. Understandably, I felt very uneasy and not a little apprehensive: however, I did manage to converse with him and challenged him to a game of cribbage. Just why I was told to sit with Doohan was a mystery then and remains a mystery now 36 years later. He could not possibly commit suicide with no braces, no belt, no shoelaces or any other item of clothing that could be utilised to kill himself. It was about 4 p.m. when Doohan, ashen-faced and very tearful, asked me: "D'you think I will hang Constable; I know I deserve to die for what I did, but I don't really want to swing on the end of that bloody rope; tell me what you think will happen Officer, I can take it."

I don't mind admitting that a full minute elapsed before I managed to reply in what I though and hoped was an impartial voice tinged slightly with optimism. After all, I couldn't possibly tell him what I really thought would happen and that I would be prepared to bet on my prediction. "It all depends on you old son." I commenced; "If you were nutty or rather insane at the time you pulled the trigger and because of that you didn't know what you were doing or perhaps you didn't realise or know that what you were doing was quite wrong, your Counsel would put that across to the Jury; the truth is old Doohan, I don't really know and neither does anyone else in this station." As it was, Doohan was hanged a few weeks later.

James Reginald Doohan

Yvonne Deighton

His trial was held at Maidstone Assizes (today they are called Crown Courts) on 23rd March, 1954. Although Doohan pleaded not guilty as instructed by his barrister Mr Cope Morgan Q.C., it was abundantly clear right from the start that the fate of Doohan was sealed. The evidence was positively overwhelming including his own confession. Mr Cope Morgan agreed that the facts of the killing were not in dispute and then he added; "I am going to say however, My Lord, that my client was insane at the time he committed the murder." He went on to outline all that I had told Doohan in his cell about insanity and whether Doohan knew what he was doing. He even called as a witness Dr Ambrose who was an Army doctor in Doohan's Army Unit in 1948; he stressed the fact that on one occasion when he examined Doohan, he formed the opinion that he was suffering from a type of schizophrenia and showed distinct signs of a split personality and he had little doubt that Doohan was still suffering from the same disorder. "For instance," said the doctor, "when I saw him in Canterbury Prison recently, he told me he had

Herbert Ketley

been having terrible headaches for a long time and was continually hearing voices; in fact he said that he heard a voice telling him to kill Ketley. He also asked me not to mention this fact in Court as he didn't want people to know that he had a screw loose somewhere." Continuing, Doctor Ambrose told the Court: "He even mentioned the Bentley murder and said - "I have killed a man, am I in the same class?"

Asked Judge Sellers: "Did YOU put the question of voices to him?" Dr Ambrose: "Yes, after he had spoken about headaches." The doctor said in reply to the prosecuting Counsel that he did not think the prisoner was certifiable under the Mental Deficiency Act. When the prosecuting Counsel Mr Tristram Beresford said to him: "Was there anything mad about going to the police and telling them the truth about this matter as he did?" Dr Ambrose: "I think he was hallucinating and acting in an incongruous manner." When Dr W. J. Gray the M.O. at Canterbury Prison was called to give evidence he made it quite clear that his diagnosis of Doohan's mental state would nullify that of Dr Ambrose.

He said; "There was no mental history of instability in the family and Doohan was an average, fairly intelligent and perfectly healthy boy at school." He added that he found no signs of insanity. Cross-examined on the possibility that Doohan was schizophrenic, Dr Gray replied; "After examining his Army medical records, I came to the conclusion that in 1948, Doohan was suffering from hysteria and was definitely malingering." In his final address to the jury, Mr Cope-Morgan realised that his client could not be saved from the gallows, reiterated everything I had told Doohan regarding the plea of guilty but insane. He told the jury that in his opinion Doohan was insane at the time of the murder and did not realise that what he was doing was wrong. However, this cut no ice with the jurors and after an absence of just over an hour, they returned a verdict of guilty as charged.

Asked by the clerk if he had anything to say before the death sentence was passed, Doohan gripped the dock rail very tightly and whispered; "Yvonne and I were in this together." This was quite untrue of course and in a clear calm tone of voice, Judge Sellars pronounced sentence of death by hanging. As he was led from the dock for the last time, Doohan scanned the faces in the public gallery and smilingly held up his clenched fists and shouted "Cheers" - This was his last desperate act of bravado. Three weeks later he was hanged.

Now, 38 years later, there are times when I see Doohan's pale conscience-stricken face appear before me and again I can hear him asking me; "Do you think I will hang Constable?" This, I fear, will remain indelibly inscribed in my memory for ever.

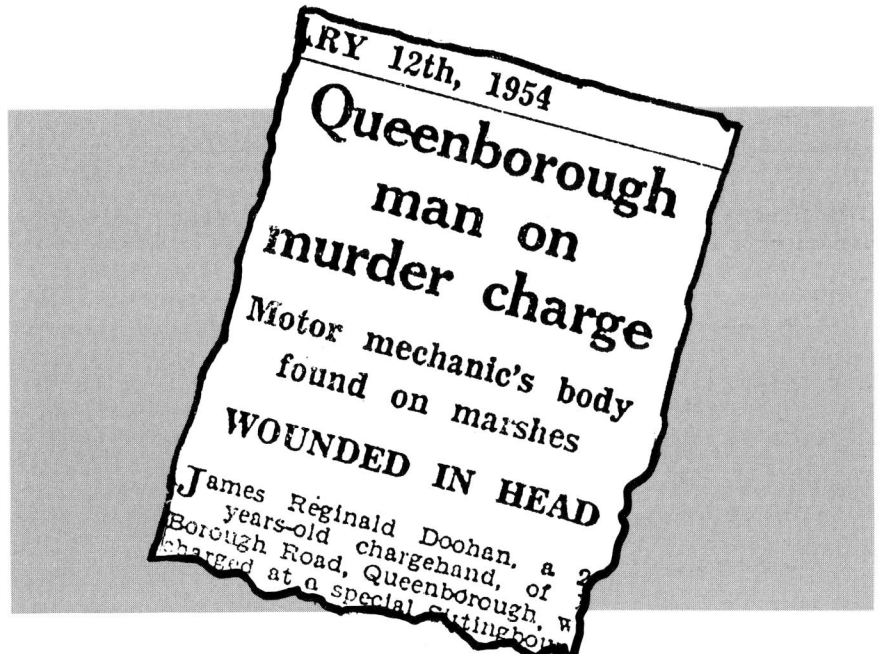

The Execution of John Any Bird Bell, age 14

At precisely 9.30 am on Friday 4th March 1831, 13 year old Richard Taylor left his Rochester home to walk the eight miles or so to Aylesford, for the purpose of collecting his father's Parish Relief grant of nine shillings. Mr Taylor was out of work and temporarily incapacitated and this meagre allowance was the sole income of the family which comprised the parents and young Richard. It was generally known that Richard collected this money and as his routine never varied, he was always home by nightfall. However, on the evening of the 4th March, he did not return home and his parents, frantic with worry, promptly informed the Parish Constable. It must be remembered that there was no County Police Force until 1857, and Parish Constables were appointed by local Justices of the Peace and other well known citizens.

With commendable alacrity, the Constable arranged for Richard's description to be circulated via hastily written posters, which were displayed in prominent positions in Rochester, the following day. At the same time it was confirmed that Richard did in fact collect the nine shillings from the Parish Relief Administrator, and he was seen to place the coins in a small, brown cloth bag. The Parish Constable also learned that on the day he disappeared, Richard was seen talking to the Bell brothers who lived nearby. The eldest boy languished under the extremely odd name of John Any Bird Bell, he was fourteen years old and his younger brother James, was aged ten.

Although there was no reason to suspect the brothers of any crime at this juncture as no body had been found, the Parish Constable did question them briefly. Both lads freely admitted having spoken to Richard, and they watched him strolling along a narrow lane which bordered a turnip field. At a later stage, a drayman delivering barrels of ale to the Blue Bell public house, recalled seeing the Bell brothers perched on a fence near the pub about 4 p.m. on 4th March. He also declared that he was quite sure that John Any Bird Bell was clutching a brown cloth bag as he sat on the fence. As the days and weeks passed, there was still no direct evidence to link the brothers with Richard's disappearance. However, on the morning of Wednesday 11th May, more than eight weeks after the boy's disappearance, John Izzard of Rochester, who was ambling through the woods at the top of Bluebell Hill, was horrified to find that he had stumbled against the partly hidden and badly decomposed body of the missing boy. He said in his evidence that he did not touch the body, neither did he examine it very closely. Had he done so, he would have observed the ugly wound in the throat of the dead child. He knew of course, that the corpse was that of Richard and it was an utterly stunned and shocked Mr Izzard, who scampered away for assistance.

Half an hour later, he returned to the scene with a handful of villagers and a very distraught Mr Taylor, who identified the body immediately. Later that day, the Bell brothers were questioned at some length by the Constable, and taken to Maidstone Prison. It was in the forbidding grey walls of the prison that the younger boy broke down and in tears related how his brother John had attacked Richard, and cut his throat with a bone handled knife, which did in fact belong to the murdered boy. Eventually, both brothers admitted that they knew Richard's movements every Friday and on the 4th March, they lay in wait for him near the woods. After luring Richard into the woods, John carried out his callous and coldly premeditated attack.

Inside the prison, James Bell having described in some detail how his brother murdered Richard Taylor, was allowed to return home but John Any Bird was charged with murder and detained. The Judges Rules and the laws of evidence prevailing today were of course non existent and the 14 year old was continually being questioned long after he admitted his guilt. John, who was an inveterate gambler when he had the money, answered the questions put to him very clearly and very calmly. When the Parish Constable asked him if Richard had pleaded for his life when he was attacked, John replied; "I do remember sir" he commenced, "that Richard sobbed bitterly and said; 'Please don't hurt me, my father knows your father; pray leave me alone and I will be good'."

But those tearful pleas for mercy were swept ruthlessly aside by the young gambler, who, goaded by the knowledge that in Richard's clenched fist was the bag containing nine shillings in silver coins, plunged the bone handled knife into Richard's throat. Following the discovery of the badly decomposed body, a local surgeon - Dr Seaton, carried out what was obviously a very brief examination of the corpse. He told the Constable that there was no need for a post mortem examination, as the cause of death was the gaping wound in the throat. Because of the surgeon's decision, the dead boy's clothes were not removed and searched; had this been carried out, the murder weapon would have been found in Richard's jacket pocket. The young murderer told the Constable that after the crime he placed the knife in the jacket pocket. On hearing this the Parish Constable obtained permission for the grave of Richard to be opened just two days after his burial and when the coffin lid was removed, the sadistic, impassive featured representative of the Law, ordered John Bell to clamber into the grave and retrieve the knife from the jacket of the now putrefying corpse. Incredibly, Bell performed this utterly nauseating chore without complaint and without any signs of flinching. In addition, not a flicker of remorse was depicted on his pallid features, as he handed the still bloodstained knife to the waiting Constable. That slimly built boy, whose cherubic countenance belied the fact that he was fourteen years old, was then returned to Maidstone Prison. I asked myself if this macabre and frightening ordeal was really necessary; but the fact remains that it did take place and the morbid, sickening details are now writ large on the pages of our not so illustrious legal history.

Above: James Bell (10) and his brother John Any Bird Bell (14) murdered Richard Faulkner Taylor (13) in the woods near where Kent's Rochester Airport now stands. John Bell was publicly hanged.

The title page of a contemporary printed account of the murder of Richard Faulkner Taylor by John Any Bird Bell.

After being taken back to prison, a prison warder, who was evidently as sadistically cruel as the Constable, placed a battered tin plate on which rested a meagre slice of bread and a large slice of cheese, on the table in front of John Any Bird Bell. "You can use the knife to cut your cheese" adjured the warder, a sardonic grin creasing his gaunt features as he laid the bloodstained knife between the bread and cheese. This harrowing experience was too much even for young Bell and he refused to eat the food.

Shortly after appearing before the local Magistrates, Bell was committed to stand his trial at Maidstone Assizes at the end of July. He was intelligent enough to realise that he would undoubtedly hang and he frequently told the Chaplain that he deserved to die on the gallows. Whether he did actually plead guilty at his trial is not recorded, but in any case the evidence and his own confession was enough to ensure that he was sentenced to death by hanging. The date set for the execution was Monday 1st August 1831 at 11 a.m. As he sat in the condemned cell, there was very little pity or even sympathy shown towards this boy; one visiting preacher called him a young assassin who had resigned himself to his fate. A local reporter, in a vain effort to impress his editor and presumably his readers, declared in his column - "The prison Chaplain has been most assiduous in his endeavours to impart religious instruction to this wretched boy and so make him ALIVE to the dreadful nature of his situation."

During his last few days in Maidstone Jail, John Bell wept frequently (which is not unusual for a child of his age), and he prayed earnestly with the Chaplain. On those occasions when his mother was permitted to visit, he clung tearfully and pathetically to her skirts. Invariably, she addressed him as "My dear tender hearted boy". One hard hearted and unfeeling prison visitor who heard her address her son in such an emotional manner, had the gall to ask her - "Why do you use such a mode of address Madam to a boy who is a convicted murderer?" "How dreadful is the sin of avarice" wrote one moronic reporter.

On Sunday, the day before his execution, Bell was said to have slept quite well and before going to bed for the very last time, he was allowed to attend Divine Service in the prison chapel. In here, he became the centre of attention as very few boys of his age were ever executed. On Monday morning, he was roused early to begin what was after all his last day on earth and he was taken to see his parents. He sobbed bitterly in unison with his mother and after a scanty breakfast, John Bell listened to a priest who prayed for his salvation and persuaded the boy to chant all the relevant penitential psalms. At the same time the prison bell commenced its grim warning of the pending execution. In his sparsely furnished cell, the ashen faced boy fell to his knees and repeatedly brushed away the almost continuous flow of tears; of his own volition, he started to pray; his voice was barely a whisper. Before he finished praying, the mournful chimes of the prison bell ceased, and simultaneously, the saturnine featured executioner, William Calcraft, who was paid a guinea for every hanging he conducted, stalked silently into John's cell. Without a word, he pinioned the boy's hands behind his slender back and led him out of the cell. Calcraft towered over John Bell as they shuffled towards the gallows near the Governor's house. The doomed boy looked imploringly around him, unable to brush away the tears that welled into his eyes and trickled down those alabaster coloured cheeks.

A surprisingly large crowd of at least four thousand, surrounded the gallows outside the prison precincts and stretched the length of Week Street; the majority of those ghouls were females who had started to congregate as early as seven a.m. The Chaplain accompanied by the Under Sheriff and the prison Governor, brought up the rear of his melancholy procession which slowly mounted the gallows platform. The Chaplain was still chanting as young John stumbled up the wooden steps. As it was not considered proper that a child so young should be observed swinging and convulsing in his death throes, a special platform had been erected which would not enable the crowd to feast their eyes on the victim immediately after the lever holding the trapdoor had been operated. The erection of this special platform was considered by the Press to be a most noble and humane gesture on the part of the prison authorities and the Magistrates.

John Any Bird Bell had stopped crying when Calcraft adjusted the rope around his neck, and was compelled to listen to the Chaplain reciting the burial service, minutes before he was launched into eternity. "Man that is born of woman" etc. Bell then seemed quite calm as he gazed at the dense throng of moronic sightseers, whose main objective was to see him hang. As John stepped forward on to the trapdoor, an uncanny silence descended on the vast crowd who came from all walks of life. A woman's wailing ruptured that strange silence and echoed along Week Street. For John Bell it was the signal for him to address the crowd. Staring unwaveringly at the sea of undulating faces, he cried out in a plaintive voice - "Pray for me, pray for a poor boy". When the Chaplain asked him if he wished to say anything else, John Bell, a convicted fourteen year old murderer, mustered sufficient strength and will power to shout to the crowd; in a shrill voice; "Now all you people, take warning by me, take warning." He was about to utter something else, when without the slightest warning, the trapdoor opened with a clatter and John Bell dropped into the aperture like a puppet on a string. Fortunately, his neck was broken instantly although the assembly could see the rope jerk and quiver for a few seconds. The body of course was not visible.

After the body had been hanging for a few minutes, it was cut down and handed over to an eager surgeon who whisked it away for dissection. To me, this was yet another bizarre and inexcusable act of barbarity on the part of our ancestors just three or four generations past.

Ironically, when Bell was first admitted to prison he was totally illiterate, but when he left his cell for the last time, he could both read and write reasonably well, thanks to the prison Chaplain. In conclusion, I find it extremely odd that at no time during his trial or in the newspaper accounts of the proceedings, was any comment made about his singularly unusual Christian names; I wonder why. In addition, very little was said about his addiction to gambling, in particular, a game called pitch and toss, which eventually led him to commit the crime of murder.

When the sea took charge.
The flooding of Margate, 1953

It is more than forty years ago now, time for memories to fade, yet the mental picture remains as clear as ever, when I think of that disastrous night of January 31st 1953. The night made unforgettable when most of the north east coast of Kent was flooded by an exceptionally high tide whipped to utter fury by a north westerly gale. Here in Kent, the towns of Whitstable, Sheerness, Herne Bay and Margate suffered the most. It was indeed a night to remember; but perhaps I should start at the beginning.

I was a policeman at the time and because of some primitive and ridiculous ruling of successive Chief Constables, I was compelled to work in Margate, even though I lived in Ramsgate. And on that memorable night, I was scheduled to be on duty from 10 p.m. until 6 a.m. This meant leaving my Ramsgate home at 9.00 p.m. in order to arrive at Margate Police Station at 9.45 p.m. My only form of transport was my pedal cycle. In those days I could not afford to buy a car on a weekly wage of £8. That four mile cycle ride in the teeth of a relentless and ever increasing gale, left me feeling somewhat dejected and temporarily exhausted when I stumbled into the Victorian Police Station in Margate's Market Square.

Nobody in the Station had the slightest inkling of what lay ahead on that awesome night, and it became abundantly clear that no significance was attached to the north westerly gale which had attained hurricane proportions. To be perfectly fair, although some police officers are considered to be reasonably omnisicient, they are not by any stretch of the imagination, aspiring meterologists. It is now clear that everyone, including the experts were caught completely off guard; no emergency plans had been formulated and the Civil Defence organisation, which was still in existence was not alerted prior to the flooding. Flood warnings were non existent in those days, quite different from the set up of today.

At 10 p.m. precisely, I left the ninety year old building, weighed down and cocooned in a bulky but very warm overcoat; to the front of this garment and attached to a wide black leather belt, was a cumbersome, heavy and totally unreliable accumulator charged lantern. Reluctantly, I plodded off into the night, heading for my Cliftonville Beat just over a mile away. At the bottom of Trinity Hill, I found myself battling against an even stronger wind the strength of which served to support my forecast of a hurricane force gale. It threatened to dislodge my helmet despite the tightly adjusted chinstrap. I could I suppose have found consolation in the knowledge that I was not struggling along on my pedal cycle for which I was paid sixpence a day for using it on police duty. I discovered that it took much more effort than usual to walk along, with the wind gusting and howling so savagely. Passing the ruins of the bomb damaged Holy Trinity Church which was demolished many years ago, I shuddered as the wind shrieked demoniacally through what was left of the shattered tower. This prompted me to quicken my step and I slowed down only when I reached the illuminated shopping area of Northdown Road, in Cliftonville.

There was not a soul in sight which I considered most unusual as, automatically, I commenced the nightly ritual of shaking hands with every shop door handle; with equal automation, I waltzed through the back alleys at the rear of the shops and tested the security of the doors. My only companions were the cats, which ran out from every conceivable hiding place. At 11 p.m. it was time for me to call the Station from No. 32 Police Box. The door slammed violently behind me as I picked up the telephone handset. Expectantly, I waited to hear the sententious tones of George Whitcomb, the only copper I ever knew to keep a silk handkerchief stuffed up his tunic sleeve; only a faint and distorted humming sound greeted my ears. This I thought, was very strange; I replaced the handset and tried again without success. After trying to phone from a public telephone kiosk, I realised then that something was wrong, radically wrong, for that too was useless.

At that time it suddenly occurred to me that in addition to having seen no pedestrians, I hadn't seen a solitary car either. Reluctantly I concluded that something was seriously wrong with our communications at least, as I met with no success in the Police Box No. 32 at the far end of Northdown Road. It couldn't be a power cut I mused as the street lights were still on. Perhaps I would see a Sergeant or an Inspector before I returned to the Station for my supper break; he would enlighten me no doubt.

By 11.30 p.m. I had checked the entire length of the shop doors on the north side of the road and scrounged the customary steaming hot doughnut from the Bakery. Here too, the amiable bakery team were unaware of what was happening or of the drama unfolding in the town a mile or so away. Ambling across to the other side of the road, I muttered goodnight to the stuffed Russian bear which stood guard behind the door of the musty smelling antique shop. Continuing to try the shop door handles, I made my way along Northdown Road towards Margate and thought longingly of that ambrosial cup of tea which would surely be awaiting me in the Station. I licked my lips in anticipation as I loped down Trinity Hill, with the wind now behind me, forcing me along. Again and again, I asked myself the same question - "Why haven't I seen one solitary person or even a car for almost four hours?" It was a complete mystery. But on reaching the foot of Trinity Hill at its junction with King Street and Hawley Street, I came to an abrupt halt, the mystery was solved. I had no alternative but to stop. For what seemed an inordinately long time, I stood rooted to the spot and not at all convinced that I was still awake or having hallucinations (I had proved some time before that it is possible to sleep standing up). But suddenly, I came to terms with stark and vivid reality. For King Street as I knew it and the crossroads no longer existed, or perhaps I should say they were not visible. Instead, there flowed a muddy

Kings Street, at the cross-roads with Trinity Hill and Hawley Street

Hawley Street looking towards Trinity Hill and pedal cycle shop

turbulent river more than three feet deep, judging by the height of the flint wall that skirted the historic Elizabethan house on the opposite corner of King Street.

The diffused light of the street lamps was sufficient to illuminate not only the fast flowing torrent but also a bizarre water carnival, gliding swiftly towards the gasworks and on to Dane Valley, where presumably it would terminate. Cardboard trays of pens and cheap wristwatches from Black's novelty shop on the seafront jostled with boxes of tools and a variety of wooden mallets from Olby's the ironmongers and a madly swirling cluster of empty beer crates.

An upturned boat and twenty feet lengths of timber wrenched from the stricken pier, inflicted tremendous damage as they were borne along by the surging flood. Almost every shop window in sight had caved in and the whole of old Margate was under several feet of water. The massive baulks of timber fell into line behind a scattered flotilla of rubber ducks and toy yachts in line ahead. It was a fantastic and apparently unending procession; why, it even had its own orchestra, conducted skilfully and indeed triumphantly by Neptune himself. I knew then that this was no dream and no venture into fantasia. Even more so when the plate glass door of Lawrence's pedal cycle shop, surrendered with a frightening crash allowing the swirling waters to lick hungrily around the gleaming roadsters and racing cycles.

Suddenly, I spotted what appeared to be the body of a small baby floating past, it had flaxen hair and was wearing a blue dress. "My God, No!" I muttered as, unhesitatingly, I waded through the icy cold water and clutched what I immediately discovered to be a pink cheeked life size doll. 'Mama' she wailed plaintively as if it was a real baby. She was still calling for Mama as I propped her up on the saddle of a toy cycle at the rear of the shop. It was then that the realisation dawned on me that to reach the Station I would have to return to Cliftonville and make a detour of at least one mile.

Feeling very cold, very wet and thoroughly miserable I was about to retrace my steps, when along the flooded King Street, a strange apparition came into view. Gradually, it materialized as the plump shape of Constable Tubby Jenkins. At the precise moment he seemed to resemble the modern day version of Buddha, but wearing a helmet and sculling a rowing boat. With miraculously acquired skill, he veered the craft towards me and came to a stop by wrapping his arms around the base of a lamp post. I was immensely glad to see old Jenks and told him so. "I won't ask you what you are doing in that boat, Jenks" I bellowed against the unceasing roar of the wind, "but I'm certainly glad to see you; I haven't seen a soul since I left the station. What's been happening and how long has this part been flooded?" "Get in and I'll tell you." he bawled as he pushed away from the lamp standard. "It started just after eleven, then the nick was flooded and the telephones went dead. The Station staff have all moved up to Divisional Headquarters in Hartsdown Road, as there's no flooding up there, too high up of course."

"What we have to do now" continued Jenkins, "is to make sure all the locals around here are awake and aware of the floods; if they want to leave, they will just

The Jetty decking, forced up from underneath

have to wait until this lot subsides, the tide is on the turn now anyway." As it happened, and as I surmised, every resident in the area was wide awake. Surprisingly, there were no casualties although one young man, who was running along the pier to warn the Station of the danger, was swept into the sea by a huge wave only to be hurled back on the pier by another such wave. I never discovered just why he chose to venture along the pier in the first place.

Just before 6 a.m. Jenkins and I rowed into the saloon bar of one of the seafront pubs where we were told that the Police Box near the Clock Tower had disappeared. We also imbibed a very large whisky and ate a delicious sandwich provided by the very kind landlady. It was 8 a.m. before I went off duty. Aided by a following wind, I cycled home to Ramsgate, and tumbled into bed. Later that day, I discovered that Ramsgate had suffered very little damage and no flooding because of its geographical position. Some days elapsed before Margate Police Station returned to normal. The town had suffered damage in excess of a quarter of a million pounds, including the loss of the old lighthouse and the destruction of the Marine Sun Deck and Westbrook Pavilion.

The people of Margate found no consolation in the pronouncement of local historians that the town received a similar but not quite so severe battering way back in 1897. And as I remarked in the opening paragraph, it was certainly an unforgettable night and one that needs no action replay.

The Great Fire of Wye 1889

On Saturday November 2nd, 1889, the Kentish Express and Alfred News allocated a whole column two feet long to one of its reporters which enabled him to describe the Great Fire of Wye. In common with most Victorian journalists, this reporter was liberally endowed with flowery language and superlatives. He informed his readers that the ancient town of Wye had suffered its biggest and most destructive conflagration in its thousand years existence. But however, it is described, this disastrous blaze destroyed or badly damaged several properties in Church Street. The value of the damage was estimated to be well in excess of ten thousand pounds; by today's standards, that sum could probably be multiplied a hundred fold. The Volunteer Fire Brigade of Ashford called it the Wye Brewery Fire in their log book and added that the details would go down in history 'in point of excessiveness'.

As expected, the full details of this terrible fire have found a permanent niche in local history. We do know that it started in a very old timber built house on the west side of Church Street, known as Cumberland House. It was flanked by the century old brewery and its outbuildings on one side and Clarabuts the draper's shop on the other. In turn the shop stood next to the three hundred year old coaching Inn - the 'Kings Head'. Many years before it was probably called the 'Saracens Head'.

There is no doubt that the fire was started accidentally, but decidedly carelessly, by a workman named Masterson, who had been working in the house, in preparation for its occupation by the son of Arthur Cumberland who owned the house and the brewery. In fact he had purchased both properties just a few weeks before. Masterson later admitted that he had been smoking in the old house and on leaving threw away a match which he thought was extinguished. He conceded that this was very foolish bearing in mind that the floor was carpeted in shavings and other inflammable materials. This occurred about 4.45 p.m. according to Masterson, and the actual ignition probably occurred about 45 minutes later. The blaze was first noticed at 6.40 p.m. and a telegram was immediately despatched to Ashford Fire Brigade some five or six miles away. However, it was 7.45 p.m. when the two horse drawn manual pump and what was called the 'steamer' pump, galloped smartly into Church Street, under the command of Captain Frank Hart. The rank of Chief Fire Officer was not created until many years later.

Long before the arrival of the Fire Brigade, Cumberland House was completely engulfed along with the malthouse, the engine house and the off-licence. This latter was a most unusual appendage for a brewery at that time. Simultaneously, the thin lathe and plaster wall dividing the house and the draper's shop, erupted into what must have been a devastating and horrendous ball of fire which completely destroyed the shop and its contents and in fact the whole building in thirty minutes. The terrified Mr Clarabut who was serving a customer at the time called to his wife who was upstairs and the three dashed out of the shop and to the other side of Church Street. From there, the Clarabuts watched in horror as their little shop built in 1620, swiftly disappeared. The terrific heat generated by the inferno could be felt even on the other side of Church Street.

The viciously gusting north east wind whipped the ever hungry flames into even greater fury and moments later, the lofty brick fronted Kings Head Hotel, was also engulfed in a sheer wall of fire. There was no escape for a building which had been the scene of many lavish functions and balls and where so many members of the aristocracy had gathered along with prominent members of the horse racing fraternity at the conclusion of Wye Race Meetings.

George Spike, the manager of the hotel, was forced to flee from the hotel leaving behind the till and its contents. By some strange twist of fate, the till was found intact the next morning. Valiantly, but always in vain, local residents and the hotel's barmaids formed a human chain stretching from the hotel to the 1869 erected village pump right outside the Methodist Chapel in Upper Bridge Street, a hundred yards away. The water filled leather buckets proved to be utterly useless as the heat was so intense that close approach to the burning buildings was quite impossible. The domestic wells soon dried up as they too were used to the fullest extent by both fire appliances. To reinforce the water supply, George Kennett and Adam Amos worked like the proverbial Trojans with their horse drawn carts, each carrying an enormously large barrel of water drawn from the river.

Soon after the arrival of the Ashford appliances, the Squire of Chilham and owner of Chilham Castle cantered into Church Street, with his own horse drawn manual pump which is still to be seen in the grounds of the castle. He had spotted the fire from Chilham and after mustering his men, who were employed on the estate, he came over on his own initiative. So quickly had the fire spread, it seemed there was a distinct possibility of it reaching the southern end of Church Street and the remaining cottages. Wisely, the owners of these cottages took the precaution of moving their valuable possessions, especially the furniture, to the other side of the street. Even there the householders property was not exactly safe with scintillating and cascading showers of red hot sparks covering every building within a half mile radius. Just after the arrival of the Chilham firemen, their Ashford colleagues discovered to their great dismay and annoyance, that their hose was much too short to stretch as far as the river almost half a mile away. The position was then so serious that it was considered expedient for the rest of the Ashford back up team to travel by special train to Wye equipped with additional lengths of hose. But the hopes of Captain Hart and his men were cruelly dashed when, after trailing the hose to the river, the pipe ruptured in several places and was beyond repair. This meant reverting to the humping of water from the carts of George Kennett and Adam Amos and the continuous refilling of the leather

The still smouldering ruins on Sunday, 27th October, 1889. The facade of the hotel is basically unchanged now

Great fire of Wye. Old village pump to right of lamp standard

buckets. And as if this was not enough, the 'steamer' broke down and an urgent message was sent to the men of the Charing Brigade for assistance. But for some still unexplained reason, the Charing firemen unanimously decided that the message was a hoax and they refused to turn out, although the glow in the sky over Wye should have been visible from Charing.

It was well past midnight when Captain Hart announced that the fire was under control, but his appliances continued to direct their hoses on to the still smouldering ruins of the four buildings for most of the following day, which of course was a Sunday. A very sad and sickening sight greeted the eyes of the hundreds of sightseers who packed into Church Street that morning. The acrid smell of burnt wood pervaded the atmosphere and wisps of smoke curled up from the embers. Only small parts of the brewery wall remained and its three tall scarred and blackened chimney stacks and the three walls of the Kings Head Hotel were silhouetted against the leaden and seemingly mournful sky; grim reminders of the savagery of that great fire. Remarkably, the only casualties were two imprudent youths from Chilham who chose to stand much too close to the burning hotel and were struck by falling tiles. Fortunately, neither was seriously hurt.

When the time came to assess the damage to property and possessions, the Kings Head Hotel sustained the greatest loss. The actual building was owned by Flints the Canterbury Brewers and was well insured with the Kent office of insurers. But the unfortunate landlord (as opposed to the manager), a Mr Sutton, the owner of a butchers shop in Chilham, was insured for a mere three thousand pounds, a fraction of his enormous loss of personal possessions and furniture. The Wye Court of Foresters lost their entire colourful regalia which was stored in a Committee room on the first floor. This was insured by the Liverpool and London Office of Insurers in the sum of one hundred pounds. The Wye Cricket Club had not bothered with insurance and lost all their cricketing gear which included some well treasured bats.

In mysterious circumstances Mr Cumberland, the brewery owner, left Wye some weeks after the holocaust and because he was never traced, despite extensive enquiries, which stretched on for many years, the land on which his house and brewery once stood, remained in Chancery for the same length of time. Eventually, in 1923, a Mr Taylor bought the land and promptly built a garage with petrol pumps. He also transferred an old aircraft hanger from the airfield in Bramble Lane and used it as a garage for his vehicles.

Today, a new block of houses occupy the sites on which the brewery and Cumberland House once stood. The old draper's shop is now an offshoot of NatWest Bank and the Kings Head Hotel, resplendent in its Victorian facade, still towers above its immediate neighbours. Ill luck has continued to plague the hotel at intervals. In 1916 a biplane from the nearby aerodrome crashed on to the roof and in October 1987, a hurricane force wind damaged two of its chimneys and severely damaged the roof on both sides of the structure.

Captain Hart and his crew aboard the 'Steamer'. The rank of Captain was the obvious choice. Fire Officers Divisional and Sub Officers were introduced many years later

In 1908, Wye had its own fire engine or to be precise, a Shand Mason Manual appliance drawn by two sturdy horses belonging to Mrs Black. The officer in charge of this first fire fighting team was George Smith, landlord of the George Inn. In 1939, Wye received its first mechanised fire engine thus replacing the ancient manual appliance. The term manual is not really misleading; about twelve men were needed to push and pull on the two horizontal wooden bars and so provided the pressure to pump water on to a fire. The 'steamer' so called because the steam needed to operate the pump came from boiling water in the cylindrical tank above the circular fire place under the tank. As a point of interest, that old 'steamer' from Ashford which performed sterling work in 1889, was later sold to the village of Bilsington. This nostalgic link with the past bought by Ashford Brigade in 1875, now nestles snugly and indeed proudly amongst a collection of veteran and vintage vehicles of all types in, of all places, the Southward Trust Museum at Paraparamau in far off New Zealand. I have ascertained that it is the grand daddy of them all in its place of honour eleven thousand miles from its birthplace. It does bear a brass plate which describes how it played a leading role in the biggest conflagration that Wye has ever known.

The Gestapo Chief of North Foreland

Because of its world famous lighthouse, its golf course and the superb unrivalled views across the shimmering waters of the Channel, North Foreland has been a favourite haunt and resting place for scores of millionaires and celebrities over the years. For instance, in 1914, John Buchan was invited to spend a few weeks of his vacation at St. Cubyn, a magnificent residence, on the esplanade overlooking the sea and a few yards from the cliff top. It was during this holiday, that he pounced on that never-to-be-forgotten title for his newly written book - the now legendary 'Thirty Nine Steps'. The inspiration for this title is reputed to be the flight of approximately 130 stone steps leading from the clifftop to the rock strewn and in parts, sandy beach, some sixty feet below. In fact, there were 78 steps in those days and they were wooden.

Just a short distance from St. Cubyn stands an even larger and possibly more imposing mansion, which bears the name of 'Naldera'. To my certain knowledge, it has borne this name for more than sixty years, a fact which I clearly recall from my boyhood days. Regrettably, from a writer's point of view, the house is now a block of flats. From the outside, however, the house looks exactly as it did in 1932, when a rather sinister German took over the tenancy with his wife and four children. His name was Doctor (a legal title) Arthur Albert Tester, who even then was a prominent Nazi, an anti semitist and a leading member of the British Union of Fascists which had an office in Broadstairs just two miles away. Tester earned the reputation of being a financial wizard commuting daily to his London office where his employees greeted him with the Nazi salute as he disembarked from his black Mercedes and strutted into the office block. According to the Press, he was a Director of several companies, one of which was financed by a high ranking member of the Third Reich, believed to be Himmler. The leaders of the Thanet Blackshirts often visited 'Naldera' and Sir Oswald Moseley with his wife Diana were sometimes seen at the house at the same time as the portly former champagne salesman Ribbentrop. Although Tester was an ardent Fascist, it is most unlikely that he organised the spate of jew-baiting in Margate in 1936.

As a gauche teenager I often walked to North Foreland on my bird nesting expeditions and somewhat dramatically I always made sure that I increased speed as I approached Naldera, especially if I saw Tester in his rose garden, which has now been replaced by garages. I knew full well that he was a suspicious character and I never lingered too long. Tester went to extraordinary lengths to cultivate the friendships of several well known and influential residents. They would never, I felt sure, reveal their identities. In 1945, one of the Thanet newspapers announced that before the outbreak of war, Tester arranged flying lessons for either his son or his nephew at Ramsgate Airport on the outskirts of the town. The true identity of

'Naldera' and its prominently placed turret room

the young man was never disclosed. For dental treatment, Tester opted for the services of Mr Morley Stebbings of Ramsgate, who later became an Army Brigadier and encountered Tester for the last time in gruesome and entirely different circumstances.

With the clouds of war gathering a few days before September 3rd, 1939, a police escort called at 'Naldera' for the express purpose of arresting Tester for internment. Not surprisingly, they found the house empty and the man who smoked cigars in a bed cocooned in black silk sheets, had disappeared. In fact Charlotte his wife and their children had returned to Germany some months before. We know for a fact that Tester left this country by sea either in his own private luxurious yacht or by U-boat; I prefer to stick to the latter. I am not alone in maintaining that after descending those stone steps opposite the house, he was rowed out to the U boat waiting off shore in the darkness. This is not so melodramatic as it may seem. His yacht, usually moored in Ramsgate Harbour would surely have been under surveillance just before the outbreak of war. Long before this, I had been told that Tester made regular contacts with U boats and other craft by signalling from the turret shaped tower on the roof of the large house. The turret had windows on three sides and was ideal for the purpose. Later, rumour suggested that a quantity of radio equipment was found in the turret.

Marianne Emig, aged 19

Just what happened to Tester after that is not quite clear. It was known that he made his way through the Balkan countries, presumably after being briefed and leaving Germany. It is an established fact that in 1944, Tester was Head of Gestapo in Rumania with his Headquarters in Castle Mintia. It is also known that when the Russian Army was advancing on Rumania, and likely to capture the Castle, Tester attempted to escape by driving through the blockade; it seems that he was shot, the car crashed into a ditch and caught fire. No doubt the charred body was soon buried because in the Autumn of 1945, our Special Branch asked the Russians in Rumania to exhume the body to have it identified by dental records and skull x-rays. By strange coincidence, the man who was given the unenviable task of identifying Tester by this means, was his old dentist, Brigadier Stebbings, newly released from a P.O.W. camp. This poses the question; why was it considered so important to have the body identified? Consequently, the Nazi who lived in Kent for more than seven years and spoke fluent English, is still buried in Rumania and remains as much a mystery in death as he was in life. There is no mention of him in the archives at Kent Police Headquarters or in the archives at County Hall, Maidstone.

Goertz (centre) and the Abwehr Agents

To clarify the position, I wrote to the Home Office and the Special Branch; I should have known better of course. No assistance was forthcoming from the German archives in Freiberrg or Coblenz. The Rumanian Embassy failed to reply to my letter; the Russian Embassy did reply but in the negative. Some time ago I went back to North Foreland and descended those dark and gloomy steps to the beach. Now, after much cogitation, I concluded that Tester's long stay in Thanet was part of a carefully planned preliminary, which would have led up to and included the invasion of this country in 1940. Make no mistake about this, if

Beach entrance or exit of the 78 steps (now 130)

Operation Sea Lion had been launched when England was still reeling from the Dunkirk disaster and our only defence was the Canadian Seventh Division based near Reigate, and our armour consisted of fifty tanks only, then the invasion would have been eminently successful; on this we must not delude ourselves. On the French coast between Calais and Cherbourg, were 39 enemy Divisions including paratroops and hundreds of tanks. There were fifteen Divisions held in reserve. Tester, with his comprehensive knowledge of southern England, would in my opinion have been Gestapo Chief for Kent and perhaps Southern England. He had been groomed for this role since 1932.

In addition, Tester was not the only agent in Thanet in 1935. Hermann Goertz, ex Luftwaffe pilot in his mid forties had volunteered to be an espionage agent and with this in mind, he rented a bungalow in Stanley Road, Broadstairs. The target for his espionage activities was Manston Air Base, having secretly sketched other military and aircraft installations in East Anglia. For transport he used an ancient motor cycle combination and was accompanied by a young woman he called his niece.

It was after the owner of the bungalow searched through his combination suit he left in the garage, that his activities were uncovered. He had returned to Germany for a few days and at Harwich telegraphed her asking her to look after his combination. He meant his motor cycle and sidecar, as he knew full well that a miniature camera was in the pocket of his greasy overalls. The evidence in the camera and his sketches of Manston were sufficient to ensure his attendance at the Old Bailey. Also found in his possessions were photographs of the aircraft carrier Ark Royal and the addresses of Nazi organisations in London. On March 4th 1936, Goertz, the son of a Deputy in the Reichstag, was sent to prison for four years. He spent most of this period in Maidstone Prison, where he met Baillie-Stewart of the Officer in the Tower fame, who was spying for Germany in 1933. He also met high ranking members of the evil I.R.A. and with them, it is conceivably possible that tentative plans for the invasion of Eire, known as 'Operation Kathleen', were spawned. Hitler had originally intended to invade Eire and use it as an additional base in the invasion of England.

Goertz was released from prison at the beginning of 1939 and back in Germany, was rapturously received by the hierarchy of the Abwehr. Goertz was then ordered to parachute into Southern Ireland in the Spring of 1940, but landed in Northern Ireland. Eventually, he made his way back to the meeting place with the I.R.A., but after several months, an informer reported him to the Irish Police. He was then interned for the duration of the war. When the war came to an end, Goertz on being told he was being returned to Germany, committed suicide by taking a cyanide tablet. He lies buried in Dublin Cemetery.

There can be no possible doubt that during his stay in Broadstairs, Goertz was in close contact with Tester but just what they planned and discussed will, I fear, never be known. When I paid a visit to 'Rosevine', the bungalow rented by Goertz, a few months ago, the owner knew nothing of Goertz or his activities. Enquiries at the block of luxury flats still called 'Naldera' elicited the fact that the tenants here knew little or nothing about the Gestapo Chief who lived there for more than seven years.

The Wrong Victim (a very strange murder)

According to a Ramsgate newspaper dated 25th February 1903, the town was 'thrilled with horror' by an appalling tragedy that occured at 14, Flora Road, just after midnight that same day. It was a small terraced house and the murder victim was William Henson aged 20 a well known and popular Ramsgate footballer; he was a bricklayer by trade. His death was caused by a tremendous explosion, which practically demolished the house and also seriously injured Samuel and Jane Henson, parents of the dead youth. However, this explosion which was heard more than a mile away, was no accident; Samuel Henson, a 58 year old foreman ganger was familiar with explosives and on that eventful and tragic night, he tried to murder his wife by using a powerful explosive called tonnite, a mixture of gun cotton and cordite.

At the time of the explosion, William Arthur Wells, a lodger with Mrs Henson and her son, was also in the house. There was another son who lived in South Africa; he was called home at once. As the story unfolded, it was made clear that all was not well with the marriage of the Hensons, although they had been married for 25 years. Samuel Henson was very quick tempered, very moody and frequently drunk; he made his wife's life a misery. He was not workshy however, and travelled extensively in the Midlands in search of work, but his contribution to the family budget never exceeded one pound a week. His son William and Wells, the lodger, paid for their keep. Before the family moved to Flora Road, they had lived in rented accommodation in Avenue Road. It was there, that Samuel Henson who had just returned from the Midlands, deliberately sought an argument with his placid natured wife Jane. He accused her of infidelity with the lodger and alleged that she purchased too many hats, eight to be precise. He also berated her for daring to enter a public house without a chaperone. So, after a thoroughly miserable Christmas, Jane Henson, her son William and Wells the lodger, took up temporary residence at 51, Plains of Waterloo, occupied by Mr Richard King, his wife and eight children. Before leaving the town to seek work in Derby, Henson went to the Kings house and threatened to kill Mr King and Jane Henson. Police Sergeant Creedy, to whom the facts were reported, took the threats seriously enough for him to instruct a constable to patrol in the vicinity of the house that same night. The next day Henson retaliated by lodging a counter complaint to Sergeant Creedy, who solemnly advised him to sober up and take his complaint to the Magistrate's Clerk.

Henson immediately reacted by bawling to the Sergeant in that quaint little police station in Charlotte Place; "I will not go to the bloody magistrates, I will finish the job myself and blow them all to hell." At his trial later that year, he denied saying this. The unfortunate Mrs Henson did in fact lodge a complaint at the Magistrate's Clerk Office and asked for advice regarding divorce proceedings.

No. 14 Flora Road today – on the left of the telegraph pole

It was just after Christmas, when Henson was working in Derby, that he wrote to his wife and begged her forgiveness and asked her to take him back. In her reply Jane Henson told him that she was applying for a Separation Order and that divorce proceedings had commenced. It was this shattering news that probably drove Henson to contemplate murdering Jane and killing himself.

He returned to Ramsgate on Tuesday 24th February 1903, and immediately made his way to 14, Flora Road, having discovered that his son had rented the house. Finding no one at home, he visited two public houses. At his trial, evidence revealed that the first pub he used was the Brown Jug, on the outskirts of the town at Dumpton. The landlord clearly remembered that Henson was carrying an oblong package about twelve inches long and seven inches wide, wrapped in a distinctive blue and white spotted handkerchief. James Sanders, the landlord, also recalled that Henson, whom he identified in Court, placed the object in the handkerchief on the window sill. Understandably, he did not question the customer about the object, as it did not seem at all significant. After consuming three pints of beer, and smoking a cigar, Henson left the pub about 4.15 p.m. Legislation restricting opening hours was not then in force. The landlady of the other public house he visited failed to identify him in Court.

About 6 p.m. Henson returned to Flora Road, where he joined his son William over a cup of tea. By then the object in the handkerchief had been placed in a well worn carpet bag together with a pair of Henson's carpet slippers. His wife, who was helping out at an old folks party, had not returned by 6.30 p.m., the time when Henson visited another public house, still carrying the carpet bag. At one stage, William asked him what was wrapped in the handkerchief; his father replied nonchalantly, "Just a few things of mine". It seems very likely that William accompanied his father to the pub, but soon returned home. It was about 10 p.m. when Samuel Henson re-entered the house, where he was met by his wife, his son and Wells the lodger. Wells in his evidence at the Assizes, declared that immediately Henson entered the house a heated argument ensued between the accused and his wife and the 'high words' continued for some time. Wells stated that it was then time for him to go to bed, not wishing to be embroiled in the argument. In his bedroom at the back of the house, he could still hear the raised voices. Then the explosion followed and a tremendous one at that and we can reconstruct the sequence of events by following the evidence of witnesses at Henson's trial, which opened at Maidstone Assizes on Monday 13th July, 1903, before the Hon. Sir Charles Darling. Mr Lowe, K.C. appeared for the prosecution and Mr Thorne Drury K.C. for the Defence. Mr Lowe asked Wells if he could enlarge on what he had overheard during that argument downstairs - Wells replied; "I heard Henson ask his wife if he could come back to live with her; but she and William the son said together - 'No, you can't, we've both had enough.' Henson then replied; 'That's it then.'"

Another important piece of evidence, which virtually sealed Henson's guilt, came from his wife; She said- "My husband was sitting down in the kitchen with the carpet bag by his side; I could see something dark coloured in the bag, which he said were his slippers. In addition to calling me a liar, he said I had been unfaithful". "It was then," she continued, "That my son William poor boy, told him to go and leave me in peace. You see, we had been arguing for some time and my husband was ranting and shouting all the time". After gentle verbal prodding from the Prosecuting Counsel, she went on a very quiet voice; "After he said 'That's it then' he stood up and lit a cigar with a fusee and then deliberately dropped the still burning fusee into the carpet bag. I realised at once that something awful was going to happen, and I screamed - 'Oh, Will, come'". It was never made clear just who she was calling as Wells the lodger was also called Will, but as her son was with her in the room, she was obviously calling for the lodger. In any case upstairs, Wells heard her call and he scrambed from his bed at once. This quick movement probably saved his life.

Downstairs, William who was standing a few feet from his mother dashed forwards, snatched the carpet bag and ran into the scullery with the intention no doubt of flinging it into the back garden. That was all the unfortunate Mrs Henson could remember at that stage. The luckless and heroic William never made it to the scullery door. The deafening explosion that occurred ensured that he died at once and there was very little left of the body. Major Cooper Key, a Home Office expert, who provisionally identified the explosive as tonnite, stated that if the explosion had occurred on the scullery floor, there would have been some noticeable signs of this on the floor.

Most of the rear of the house was demolished by the terrific blast, all the windows were blown out and the bed used by Wells, was found in the rubble. Wells had clung to a drainpipe when he felt the floor giving way. The next day two large axes, owned by the Hensons, were found embedded in the roof of a house in Dane Road, more than a hundred yards away. When Constable Barrow heard the detonation, he thought at first that a maroon had been fired to summon the lifeboat crew. He took just a few minutes to locate the house, where he was met by a thoroughly shocked Wells and a crowd of bewildered and frightened neighbours. Aided by the weak light of his bulls eye oil lantern, he scrambled through the rubble and found Henson sitting on the kitchen floor; he was covered in dust and debris. His wife was lying on her side a few feet away with both legs trapped by a large settee; they were both seriously injured. It was after Barrow had dragged Henson into the remains of the passage near the shattered front door that he noticed a deep gash about three inches long across his throat. Barrow concluded that this injury had been inflicted after the explosion, as there was no dust on the blood and yet Henson was completely covered in dust. At that stage, he was joined by Sergeant Creedy and both grabbed Henson when they saw him trying to tear his wound open even further.

With the arrival of more policemen, Henson was restrained until he and his wife were taken to hospital by ambulance. In the darkness, the police officers failed to notice that Jane Henson also had a deep cut on her throat together with numerous cuts on her arms and chest. At the hospital the House Surgeon - Dr Norris Stevens, thought her scalp wound had been caused by falling debris. However, he was quite sure that the throat wounds of both, were made by the blade of a knife. Constable Barrow corroborated this to a certain extent, when he told the Court how he found a bloodstained penknife, later identified as Henson's, in the rubble, a few feet from the place where Henson had been sitting. Dr Stevens remained unmoved in his opinion that a knife caused the throat wounds and deep cuts and scratches on Jane Henson's arms and chest. All the wounds, he said, were consistent with the knife produced in evidence.

The prisoner remained on the critical list for some days, guarded constantly by a policeman. When he was told that William his son had been killed, he commented; "I'm very sorry for my poor boy, I never meant it for him, it's a pity she hasn't gone with three or four more of them; if she'd stayed at home, this wouldn't have happened." Mr Drury, for the Defence tried to discredit the evidence of Sergeant Creedy and P.C. Ewell, who had both questioned Henson at his bedside. In this, however, he failed as both officers refused to change their testimonies. Neither side commented on the grotesque appearance of Henson whose scalp was swathed in bandages and plasters; no mention was made of his second suicide attempt when he dashed his head against the wall of his cell.

When Henson was cross examined by Mr Lowe, he readily admitted that he took the explosive into the house in his carpet bag, but he had no idea that it was fitted with a fuse and detonator when he bought it from a man called Green in Chatham (he was never traced). Oddly enough, Henson was not asked just why he took the explosive into the house and he could not explain the presence of a spare detonator in his coat pocket. Because of his throat wound which he had inflicted

Above: The back of the house shortly after the explosion.
(Drawn by Ann Sutherland)

TERRIBLE TRAGEDY AT RAMSGATE.

FOOTBALL PLAYER KILLED.

House Wrecked by an Explosion.

MAN AND WOMAN FOUND WITH THEIR THROATS CUT.

MYSTERIOUS AFFAIR.

Ramsgate was thrilled with horror in the earlier hours of this morning with the story of an appalling and unique tragedy—involving the death of a promising young workman named William Henson, terrible injuries to his father and mother, and the partial destruction of a dwelling-house, by an as yet unexplained explosion. Some mystery enshrouds the horror, but the main facts seem to be these —

Above: William Henson, the son murdered by mistake

Above: The accused, Samuel Henson, from a sketch made in court.
(Drawn by Ann Sutherland)

himself, he spoke in almost a whisper. He denied having dropped the burning fusee into the carpet bag deliberately and maintained that it was a tragic accident. He could not recall the explosion as 'everything went black'. He also vehemently denied attacking his wife in the darkness and cutting her throat, when he discovered that she was still alive after the blast. Mr Drury, well aware that his chances of proving his client innocent were virtually nil, made a moving and eloquent plea to the jury.

Predictably, his pleas were in vain and the jury took just a few minutes to return a verdict of 'guilty'. When asked by the judge if he had anything to say, the prisoner answered 'No'. The dreaded black cap was placed on the head of the judge as he passed sentence of death in the customary and impersonal manner. Henson remained unmoved and stared blankly at the judge before being led away. Not everyone in the town agreed with the verdict and a petition for leniency was launched by Dr Nichol, the family's G.P. As expected the appeal was successful on the grounds that Henson was insane when he committed the dreadful act. His Counsel, Mr Thorne Drury, should have put this plea of guilty but insane to the jury in the first instance as the evidence against Henson was overwhelming.

In conclusion I feel sure that those townsfolk who launched the petition for clemency ninety years ago were fully justified in doing so. They undoubtedly saved a demented man from the gallows, to which he would have been taken within two weeks of his being sentenced to death.

Rape and Murder on the Black Path

About 6.45 p.m. on Tuesday August 22nd 1944, 15 year old Betty Dorian Pearl Green, left her home in Newtown, Ashford, Kent and met up with her best friend Peggy Blaskett to go to the fair in Victoria Park. Not unexpectedly, it wasn't long before they made the acquaintance of two young men; they were members of the United States Air Force, stationed a few miles from Ashford and attached to the 306th Fighter Control Squadron. It was generally thought that American servicemen were much more charming and exciting than their British counterparts, as well as having a lot more money to spend and possibly the odd pair of nylons to give away, usually as an inducement to encourage sexual manouvres. Betty, by far the more daring and adventurous of the two girls, started kissing her partner, but the more reserved Peggy, held back.

They were all enjoying themselves however, and it wasn't until around half past nine, that Peggy decided that she had had enough and returned home. Betty stayed in the park for nearly an hour after her friend returned home to Francis Road some 400 yards from the park and fairground. Betty left the park on her own at 10.20 p.m. As she strolled down Newton Road which runs parallel with the main railway line into and out of Ashford Station, it was quite dark and being wartime there were no street lights, the blackout forbade that of course. She passed young Leslie Champion who cycled past her shouting a cheery "goodnight Betty". Just about that time, Corporal Ernest Lee Clark and Private Augustine Guerra, had been enjoying themselves in the public bar of the 'Smiths Arms' some five hundred yards away across the fields on the right hand side of Newtown Road. They were both rather drunk on the strong bitter ale which in 1944 was still rationed. The two airmen were making their way to Newtown Road and then to the Rail Station it appears and to accomplish this they had to walk along the Black Path, so called because of its total lack of illumination in either direction. It was a rather desolate place at the best of times anyway. By a strange coincidence, one of the locals in the bar of the Smith's Arms was William Green, Betty's father. In fact he watched the two Americans leave the pub. In common with many British men living near American bases, he had mixed feelings about some of the Allies. Women always seemed to respond to the Yanks, which in the main was due to the spending power of our visitors. But they were still our Allies and therefore entitled to some sort of respect.

Green himself did not leave the pub until closing time and in any case staggered home along a little used footpath to the right and behind the Smith's Arms. Had he chosen to use the Black Path route, he might conceivably have heard the pitiful groans and whimpers coming from behind the six foot high fence made of railway sleepers which lined the path for some considerable distance. As it was, she was probably dead before he arrived home. When those two Americans, hit by the cool refreshing night air, were nearing the end of the Black Path at its junction with Newtown Road, they made out the outline of the slimly built Betty Green, heading towards her home to the right of the two men. They called to her and on recognising the accents she relaxed and feeling reassured slowed her pace. Betty liked Americans; she liked their banter, their slang and also because they always listened to her when she was talking, quite unlike the British lads.

Clark and Guerra soon caught up with her and having met her before both men knew that she was but a child. Betty started flirting even at school, but was still very naive. Precisely at what stage she realised that she was in danger as the two men approached, will never be known. But she was in no doubt of their intentions when they forced her back along the path and pushed her through a gap in the fence with a hand rammed roughly and tightly over her mouth and held there, and at the same time she was forced to the ground. Betty Green had grown up in the belief that men are the natural protectors of women and she also believed that the American servicemen were the friends of all British girls. How wrong she was On that tragic night Betty Green learned the real truth as she was pinned on the damp grass behind the high fence.

Meanwhile William Green, her father, had arrived home where his wife greeted him in despair. Observing the anguished look on her face he asked; "Betty not home yet then?" "No, she isn't and I'm worried," replied Mrs Green tersely. William Green, obviously not sure if his wife was telling the truth, dashed upstairs to Betty's room which was, of course, extremely untidy with clothes scattered over her bed and even on the floor. Conceding that his daughter was not home, and there was no sign of her, he went downstairs very slowly and very thoughtfully. Mrs Green was then waiting at the bottom of the stairs with her coat and hat on, drumming her fingers on the stair rail. "Perhaps she's gone to the Blasket girl's house in Francis Road," she said and without any further exchange, they walked hurriedly to Francis Road, about a mile away. It was then well after eleven o'clock and the Blaskets had retired early to bed on that night. This did not worry Mr Green, he banged loudly and furiously on the front door until Peggy's father came to the door sleepily rubbing his eyes. When Mr Green explained the reason for the late call, Peggy was called from her bed; she was shocked to hear that Betty had not returned home, but could throw no light on her absence. She explained how happy they had been in the company of two American airmen and when she left Victoria Park, Betty was still with the men. She omitted the fact that Betty had been rather intimate with one of the men. She also failed to add that Betty had something of a reputation with the younger members of the other sex; in fact Peggy left early as relations with the two Yanks were going too far, in her estimation. She left this aspect out as well. She concluded by telling the Greens that the two Americans seemed "nice, just like gentlemen."

At this worrying stage, Mr and Mrs Green hurried off to the Ashford Police Station in Tufton Street, to report their daughter as missing. Although the parents

The Black Path, Newtown

held out some hope that she may have gone home during their absence, the fact that she had been seen with the two Americans, who were older than Betty worried them considerably. The Station Officer making out the missing person form tried to reassure the Greens. He advised them to go home and wait as she would probably turn up soon. It was only midnight and headstrong youngsters often did this sort of thing, not realising the pressure and worry they were causing their parents. The police officer did tell the parents that a search for Betty would be organised at first light unless he heard from them that Betty had returned home.

Dejected and extremely worried Mr and Mrs Green returned home, passing within yards of the crumpled body of their young daughter behind the fence of the Black Path. On reaching home, William Green wanted to look for Betty using a torch, but where did he start? Realising the utter futility of this, he and his wife sat huddled up in their sitting room, fully expecting to hear Betty knock on the front door. Tearfully, they discussed their lack of responsibility in allowing a fifteen year old girl to have so much liberty. But recriminations were utterly useless, they both knew that and they both turned to prayer. Their prayers were not answered however. At 7.15 a.m. on August 23rd, one of the gangers working on the railway line near the Newtown Bridge, overlooking the Black Path (see photograph), spotted the girl's body lying near the fence of the Black Path. Even from that point the men guessed and quite rightly that she was dead, lying in a peculiar curled up position. Her clothes were disarranged and immediately, the police were notified. Within two hours the area was cordoned off and Dr Keith Simpson, the Home Office pathologist was making a preliminary examination before the body was removed to the mortuary behind Ashford Hospital.

On conducting a post mortem examination, he collected scrapings from under the girl's fingernails and hair samples from her clothes. Semen stains on her skirt were analysed and found to belong to two different blood groups. Severe bruising

The murder victim, Betty Green

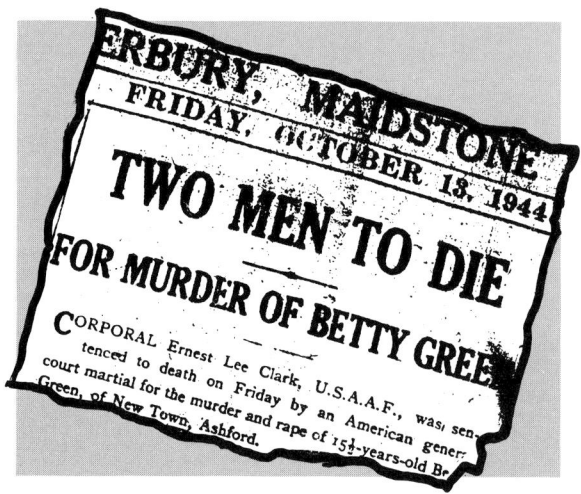

on her neck was consistent with having been manually strangled and injuries to the lower parts of her body indicated that she had been subjected to an attack of unusual ferocity, carried out after the young girl had stopped struggling. A policeman informed the Greens that Betty's body had been found and regretfully asked them to accompany him to the mortuary for one of them to identify Betty's body. They both knew that the body would be that of Betty, immediately they saw the clothes.

Predictably, the hunt switched to the American air base a few miles from Ashford. Police activity on the base became very intensive and the Military Police were most co-operative and soon organised an identification parade. By then the time of Betty's death had been established as around 10.30 p.m. on Tuesday and William Green recalled seeing the two tipsy Americans leaving the Smith's Arms; he was asked to pick out the two men. Leslie Champion, the last person other than the killers to see Betty alive, came forward with the information about his saying goodnight to Betty about 10.20 p.m. the night before. He shuddered to think that a few minutes later she was brutally raped and murdered.

Peggy Blaskett was also asked to identify the two men she and Betty had met in the Park. She was very uncertain but William Green had no hesitation in picking out Clark and Guerra. Their clothes were examined for forensic evidence and samples of semen stains on their trousers were compared with the samples found on the dead girl, they matched. Further damning evidence against the pair was then discovered. Guerra's scalp bore scratches and hair found on Betty's skirt was identical to his. A clump of Clark's hair had been pulled out during the struggle and traces of it were found under Betty's fingernails.

The provisions of the American Visiting Forces Act 1942, allowed commanding officers to arrange Courts Martial for those accused of serious crimes to be held local to the scene of the crimes. So it was that the trials of both men

Black Path where it joins Newtown Road. The body was behind the fence, near the car

were held in the Ashford Town Council Chambers (now a hairdressers opposite Woolworths). Private Augustine Guerra was sent for trial on September 24th, 1944: His unsworn statement was read out to the officers forming the Court Martial; "The only thing I can say is I was drunk and did not know what I was doing. When I get drunk, I lose my mind or something. I never done something like this before; I will not believe the girl is dead. If I thought I had killed the girl, I would have it on my nerves, but I haven't. On that night I had plenty to drink and I was drunk." Captain Todd, prosecuting, said that Guerra was still legally responsible for his actions. He pointed out that Guerra could not have been so drunk, he did not know what he was doing. His statement showed he had had his mental faculties.

Captain Correla defending, pleaded that there was no evidence of malice aforethought and asked for a plea of involuntary manslaughter. But as there was overwhelming evidence of forcible rape, it was a very weak plea indeed. The members of the Court took 15 minutes to find Guerra guilty as charged and to sentence him to death by hanging.

Corporal Ernest Lee Clark, tried just under two weeks later had dictated a statement to Lieutenant Freedman. Parts of his statement were read out to the officers. Freedman added that Clark had told him prior to the officially made

Albert Pierrepoint, the Public Hangman

statement; "I know I'm guilty of rape but as far as the murder's concerned, I didn't do it." Clark's statement went further than Guerra's had, although it confirmed the salient points. "Me and Guerra had been drinking heavily and when we reached the end of the Black Path, I stopped the girl". The statement went on to describe how they dragged her into the field and Clark admitted aiding and abetting Guerra in raping the unfortunate girl. He insisted however, that when they left her, her heart was still beating and he could feel a pulse which he thought was still strong. Captain Correla requested that the Court should return a verdict of statutory rape and manslaughter, but this too failed to impress five lieutenant colonels and a major who formed the Court Martial. They found Clark guilty on all specifications and sentenced him to death by hanging.

Albert Pierrepoint, Britain's legendary hangman, was hired to execute the sentences at Shepton Mallet Prison. He openly criticised the American custom of making the condemned men stand on the platform under the noose for fully five minutes while a senior officer recited the charges against them. What should have taken only a minute under British law, was a long drawn out tortuous procedure under the American system. Pierrepoint also considered it totally bizarre that prior to the hangings, a Bacchanlian orgy in the form of a feast and buffet, was laid on for the officials and prison staff, particularly as the hangings were scheduled to take place at 1 o'clock in the morning.

It is interesting to note that more than four hundred members of the American armed forces were tried and sentenced to death in the European theatre of war for crimes ranging from rape, murder, desertion and attacking senior officers. At Shepton Mallet Prison, 17 were hanged during the period of hostilities and two faced the firing squad. Of those seventeen hanged, Albert Pierrepoint despatched thirteen to eternity and his uncle Thomas hanged the other four.

Murder in the Village School

The charming village of Biddenden nestling deep in the heart of rural Kent, has long been renowned for its association with the legendary Siamese twins known as the Biddenden Maids. In the year of 1899, however, the spotlight of publicity was focused on the village for an entirely different reason. This was a cunningly planned and bizarre murder that completely stunned the twelve hundred parishioners. It was perpetrated by none other than the most unlikely of females, the middle aged daughter of the Rector of Biddenden. It was also carried out in the most unlikely of places, the village school. The unfortunate victim was John Whibley, the village shoemaker who, with his wife Sarah, lived above his tiny shop in the High Street right next to the local school. A Sunday School teacher, he was a very religious man who was held in great esteem by the villagers; that is until 1897 when an ugly rumour swept through the village indicting him as one who had indecently assaulted a young girl, a member of his Sunday School class.

This evil rumour was initiated by the other Sunday School teacher, Bertha d'Spaen Peterson, the rector's daughter. Now, this tall elegant and rather plain looking woman who was also a keen horsewoman and rode to hounds, became insanely jealous of Whibley's popularity in the Sunday School and frequently, she deliberately chose to quarrel with him regarding the supervision of the School. John Whibley, invariably a placid man, realised he had cultivated an enemy, when he read the contents of a nasty vitriolic letter she sent him. This letter was read out at the trial; in it, Bertha wrote; "You have committed an atrocious crime against God and against a child." This was quite untrue and emphatically denied at the trial by John Whibley's grieving widow. Bertha let it be known that she believed he was guilty and in fact added another lie stating that John had paid an unknown person the sum of five pounds as hush money. This too was never substantiated but the hypocritical and fawning church dignitaries chose to support Miss Peterson's story as did some of the simple minded villagers. Eventually poor John Whibley was compelled to resign from the post at the Sunday School and this really hurt him.

Although it was well known in the village that Bertha was decidedly eccentric and mentally deranged (not all there was the expression), her mental state was conveniently side tracked. And yet on several occasions, she was seen walking through the High Street attired in only her dressing gown and some other flimsy apparel. It was generally supposed that her mental aberrations started when tragically, her mother was severely burned when she stumbled on to the drawing room fire in the rambling old Rectory. As a result, she died soon afterwards. Some time after the old lady's death, some of the more influential parishioners noticed that the ageing Rector was being sadly neglected by Bertha who was then

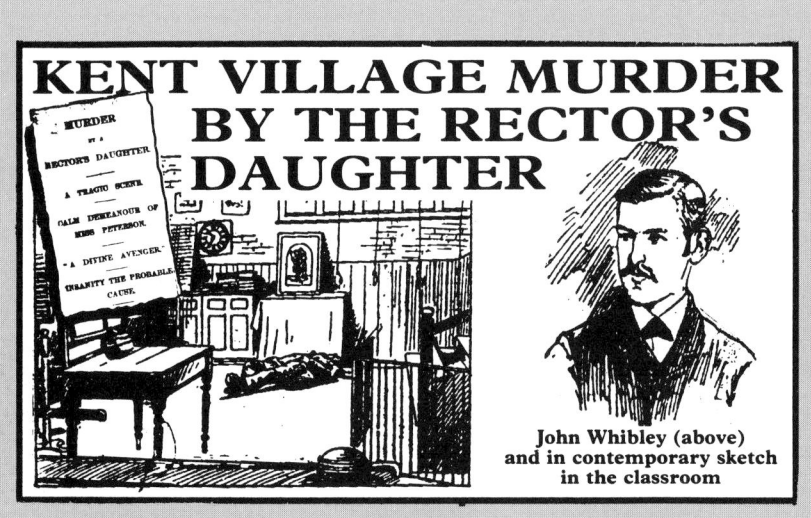

John Whibley (above) and in contemporary sketch in the classroom

42 years old. In fact they were so concerned they quietly removed the old man from his home and choosing a time when Bertha was known to be in church. He was taken to nearby Cranbrook and eventually moved to Devonshire where he spent his last days. When Bertha discovered that her father was missing, she mounted her pedal cycle and pedalled furiously and no doubt angrily towards Cranbrook. However, her journey was cut short when her cycle sustained a puncture and still seething, returned to Biddenden.

Long before she left the village after her father's death, it became painfully clear that her mental condition was rapidly deteriorating and this, together with what was termed her religious mania, fanned her obsessive hatred of John Whibley, who as a cripple always used a walking stick to get around the village. He was very relieved when she suddenly left Biddenden and rented a cottage called 'Hillside' in Egerton some eight miles away. She used the cottage infrequently and always accompanied by her friend Miss Gould. She continued to rent the cottage when she obtained employment as a nursing sister in an institute for female inebriates near Reigate. This strange establishment bore the title - 'Lady Henry Somerset's Industrial Farm Colony.'

On the occasions she returned to her cottage at Egerton, during 1897 and 1898, she caused considerable alarm in the village, when she was seen firing a Colt revolver in a 'shaw' (small wood) near her cottage. Her target was a flat piece of wood wedged vertically into a hedge. The local grocer confessed that he had given her this plank of wood and was very puzzled as to why she required it. Later, this plank was found to contain at least forty bullet holes, most of which indicated that the revolver had been fired from a close range. She carried on with

The Rose Inn, Biddenden

her target practice whenever she visited the cottage, until the day arrived when she considered that she was reasonably proficient.

On Wednesday 1st February, 1899, this strange woman telegraphed Mrs Stapley the landlady of the Rose Inn on the main road at Biddenden, and booked a room for herself and not Miss Gould. After settling in her room at the Inn, she made unexpected visits to three persons with whom she was not on good terms when she left the village. Those concerned were Mr Pinyon and Mr Lavence, both churchwardens and Miss Thirkell, a church worker. Bertha, they all agreed, had been openly hostile to them in the past and they were very surprised at the attitude she displayed when she visited them. It was an attitude which they considered was charming and disarmingly affable, in complete contrast to her demeanour of the past. She invited the three to be present in the John Mayne School after church on Sunday morning 5th February, to watch her presenting a picture of Christ as the Good Shepherd to the school.

All three regarded this invitation with much scepticism and more than a hint of suspicion, bearing in mind her past treatment of them. As it turned out, not one of the three kept the appointment at the school; two cried off because of the weather and the other through illness. Dame Fortune must have smiled benignly on Messrs Pinyon, Lavence and Miss Thirkell, as, at Bertha's trial, it was considered extremely likely that they all figured largely on her 'hit list'.

On Saturday evening 4th February, Bertha wrote a letter to the luckless John Whibley; the letter was very apologetic and in it she told him of her intention to retract all the evil things she had said about him two years before. She invited John to be at the school on the Sunday morning and mentioned that the two

Whibley's house in 1899, still the same today

churchwardens, Miss Thirkell and the Reverend Mr Raven would be at the school as well. Mr Raven had taken over the living when old Mr Peterson died. Bertha asked Mrs Stapley, to make sure that the letter to Whibley was delivered that very night, as indeed it was by Mrs Stapley's youngest daughter. In her evidence, Mrs Stapley recalled that Bertha had brought with her, the nursing uniform from the Home for alcoholics at Reigate. She added that she helped Miss Peterson to wrap the picture of Christ, which Bertha informed her would be presented to the school on Sunday morning.

Mr Raven also received a written invitation to attend the school after church on Sunday morning; why she didn't ask him personally remains a mystery, as he did in fact ask her to play the organ during the Service; she said she would be only too pleased to do this. The thoroughly perplexed Whibley did not know what to make of his letter, especially as the envelope contained two half sovereigns to be given to the Free Foresters of which he was a member. In the last paragraph she wrote; - "I would like to meet you in the school, shake hands and forgive and forget." At the trial, Sarah Whibley deposed that after getting over his initial surprise, John was delighted to know that Bertha was retracting her nasty allegations after all this time.

With unpredictable irony, Bertha and John found they were kneeling side by side at Holy Communion on that fateful Sunday morning; even as she knelt, some of the worshippers behind Bertha noticed that her right hand strayed constantly to her right hand pocket of her coat and the pocket seemed to bulge rather ominously. It needed no great degree of logic to conclude just what was in the pocket. After the Service Whibley limped home a few yards away for a few minutes before entering the school and the Rector went straight across the road into the school and entered the nominated classroom. On top of the old harmonium stood the exquisitely engraved picture of Christ the Good Shepherd. On entering the room John Whibley placed his hat and stick on a table near the door.

Significantly, the other three she had invited were not present. In his deposition at the trial, the Reverend Raven stated; "Miss Peterson greeted us and then said to John; 'Please look well at this picture'; that was all she said. The unsuspecting Whibley, possibly shrugging aside for the moment all recollections of the past and Bertha's mental instability, limped across the floor to the harmonium. As he bent his head to examine the picture, Bertha Peterson produced the revolver from her pocket, placed it a few inches from John's ear and pulled the trigger. Before the echo of the shot died away, poor John Whibley slumped to the floor with blood gushing from his ear; he never had a chance to examine that picture and he was dead before he fell to the floor in an ever widening pool of blood still oozing from his head. The horrified Rector who did not actually see the shot fired, did see Bertha standing over John still holding the smoking Colt revolver. He fled from the room without a word, no doubt to summon assistance. In the playground he collided with Mr Houghton, the schoolmaster who lived next door and had heard the shot and ran out to investigate. "She has shot John Whibley" blurted the still trembling Rector. As Mr Houghton walked into the classroom, Bertha calmly handed him the revolver saying; "You can have this now, I had to do it to protect the children." Then with head held high, Bertha strolled nonchalantly from the room, into the playground and turned right into the High Street. It took the still dazed Mr Houghton a few seconds to realise what had happened before he composed himself and ran after the angular woman attired in black. Enlisting the aid of Priffon Avery, who lived on the right hand side of the school drive entrance, and was the village harness maker, they ran after Bertha and guided her gently into the public bar of the Chequers Inn directly opposite the school entrance. Meanwhile the Rector had summoned the village doctor Hele-Bate, who examined the body and pronounced life extinct. As they waited in the Inn for the arrival of Constable Mungham, the local policeman, Bertha whispered to Priffon Avery; in a controlled voice; "You know of course that a woman is justified in killing a man."

When Constable Mungham arrived and recovered from the initial shock, he soon assessed the situation which was abundantly clear in any case, and after examining the body, he telephoned Cranbrook Police Station and asked for assistance and transport. By that time the landlord had ushered them all into his private quarters as his public bar was soon filled with goggle eyed spectators. In reply to the formal questioning by the Constable, Bertha replied; "Where have you gentlemen been to allow that man to outrage little children?" Later, a search of her room in the Rose Inn revealed 43 rounds of .32 ammunition; there were five more rounds in the chamber of the Colt.

Right: Miss Peterson

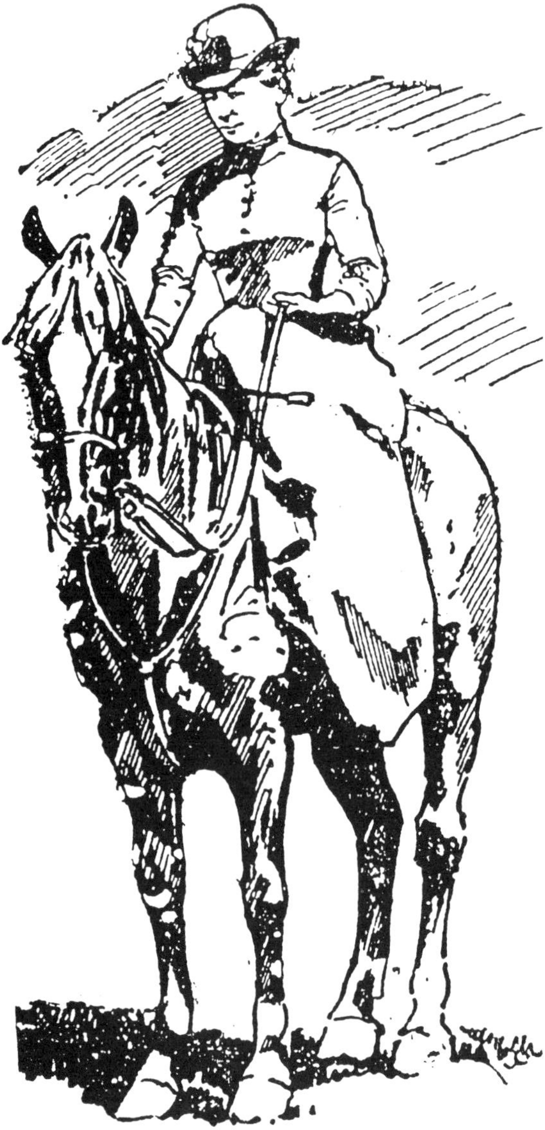

Below: The Target, upon which Miss Peterson practiced with her revolver at Egerton

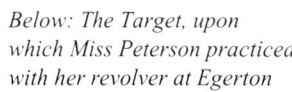

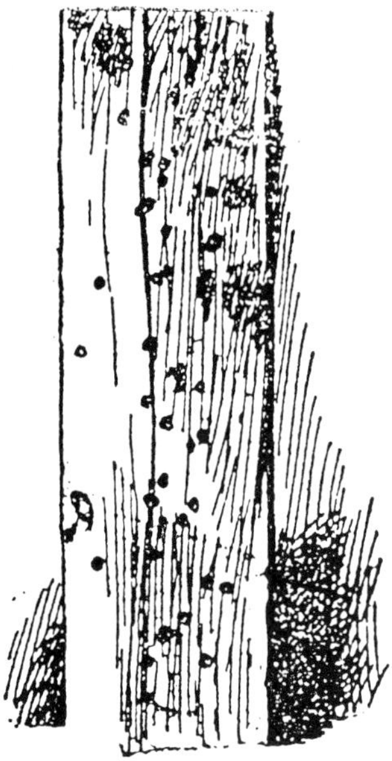

When she arrived at Cranbrook Police Station, she seemed quite rational and Superintendent Thomas Fowle solemnly charged her as follows; "That on Sunday 5th February, 1899 at the hour of 11.30 a.m., you did feloniously and with malice aforethought kill John Whibley by shooting him with a revolver." He cautioned her and she answered; "I shot him".

A post mortem examination was carried out by Dr. Joshua Kerr Law, who deposed at the inquest and at the trial. "The bullet entered the brain through the right ear and in my opinion that was the cause of death." Following the inquest Dr

Kerr arranged to have the body repositioned on the classroom floor in exactly the same position as it was originally. This was probably for the benefit of the Jury who were all villagers and who had to view the body. The inquest was held on Monday afternoon 6th February and the school was closed for the day. Mr C. D. Murton was the Coroner and he told the Jury that there was only one possible verdict they could return, which of course they did.

From the moment she was arrested until she was arraigned at Maidstone Assizes where she was found guilty but insane, Bertha Peterson displayed not the slightest trace of remorse or regret. The vacillating mental state of this tragically pathetic creature was evident for all to see throughout her trial and the prolonged preliminary hearings in the Magistrates Courts. At one of those hearings, she clutched a faded posy of wild flowers tightly to her bosom. Predictably, she spent the rest of her life behind the grim forbidding walls of a lunatic asylum. Bertha Peterson died in that asylum or mental hospital as it is called today when she was well past the age of ninety. Throughout her long stay, it is doubtful whether she knew or even appreciated just where she was, or what was going on around her.

From what I could gather, very few villagers in Biddenden knew anything about this murder that took place more than ninety years ago. The current hosts of the Rose Inn where Bertha stayed, were quite unaware that Bertha had stayed there prior to the murder; the landlord of the Chequers Inn knew nothing about it either. On visiting the John Mayne School I was privileged to be allowed to examine the school log book, in which Mr Houghton had written in beautiful copperplate; "the school was closed today 6th February 1899 (the day of the inquest) because of a terrible accident which befell one of the villagers." The exterior of the school has changed slightly and the classroom has been altered by repositioning the door and the window. Whether it was intentional or not I do not know, but the floor of the classroom was painted a deep red and has been so for many years. The attractive little cottage in which the Whibleys lived all those years ago is still there. Again, the present occupants knew nothing about that terrible tragedy, neither had they heard of John Whibley; however, they did tell me that when they moved in some years ago, they did find in the attic a quantity of leather pieces - the sort of leather that a cobbler would use on his last. Now they know just who owned that leather.

The Murder of Caroline Trayler
(A guilty man goes free)

Caroline Ellen Trayler had just attained the enchanting age of eighteen when she married Sergeant Edgar Trayler of the Durham Light Infantry in the autumn of 1942. He was stationed near Folkestone as were so many of our troops and in the Spring of the following year, he was posted to North Africa to serve in the long running desert campaign. If one is tempted to ask why a girl should marry at so tender an age, it would be as well to recall that thousands of girls did exactly the same, whether they were genuinely in love or not, before their husbands were sent abroad - some never to return. Caroline was a very pretty girl and knew it; she was also very naive and did not know it. Husband Edgar at the age of 22, was much more mature and probably missed her more than she missed him during that first eventful year.

Caroline was an usherette in the Central Cinema in Folkestone, living with her parents Mr and Mrs Stapleton at 3, Sussex Road. Not surprisingly, Caroline was still very fond of male company and after the end of the evening performance on Whit Sunday 17th June, 1943, at nine-o-clock she sauntered into the public bar of the Mechanics Arms, a few minutes walk from the cinema. She bought half a pint of beer when most girls would have preferred spirits such as gin or port and lemon. Sure enough, it wasn't very long before she was spotted in that packed bar and she was approached by a powerfully built and reasonably good looking soldier who had been sitting near her table with his friend, Bombardier Knight. Gunner Denis Edmund Leckey was 24 years old and married with a wife and two children in Manchester; in addition, he was convinced that he was God's gift to women. Invariably, he succeeded in convincing unsuspecting girls that indeed he was such a gift. After a few minutes, Leckey's mate Bombardier Knight conceded that three amounted to a crowd and left the pub.

Caroline's visit to the pub that night was also her last; shortly after leaving the pub together, they strolled along Ford Road, it was still daylight and no doubt Leckey had just one object in mind. It was still daylight when several passers by saw them enter an empty shop not far from Sussex Avenue where the doomed girl lived. Exactly what happened in that gloomy and dusty interior we will of course never know. We do know however, that once inside Leckey viciously attacked Caroline by raping and strangling her. Callously, he left her body there where it was found later that week on Thursday 21st June. Before leaving, he stole her wedding and engagement rings; oddly enough, he did not steal from her handbag which was later found nearby by a patrolling policeman. Leckey did not catch the transport laid on to return men on leave back to camp. At that time, he was it seems, still in the shop. Arriving back in barracks at 1.30 a.m., he was reprimanded by the Sergeant of the Guard, after making the excuse of having met a W.A.A.F. officer and offering to carry her suitcase; all untrue of course.

The next morning, Mr and Mrs Stapleton, alarmed by Caroline's failure to return home reported their daughter as a missing person to Folkestone Police. In the Army base, Leckey appeared to be very nervous and was told repeatedly to pull himself together. On Tuesday, 19th June, he made the mistake of asking a barrack room mate; "Have you heard about the murder, the woman who was murdered I mean, it was in the papers today, I think." As the body was not discovered until Thursday 21st June, this was defined as valuable evidence for the prosecution at Leckey's trial. On Wednesday, June 20th, Leckey hurriedly left the barracks with a leave slip bearing the forged signature of his Company Commander. He also stole several paybooks and a quantity of cash and then made his way by train to his home in Manchester. He told his family that he was on embarkation leave before being sent overseas.

It was during the morning on Thursday, 21st June, that the crumpled body of Caroline was found by one of the Police search party. Their fears for her safety had been well founded. A full description of Leckey was circulated countrywide. Leckey, realising of course that Police would call at his home, suddenly departed on Friday 22nd June, leaving behind his Army uniform including his thick fibre khaki shirt. One can only speculate on the excuse he made to his wife and mother for leaving so soon. Leckey travelled by train to London and during the journey, conversed with Mrs Woolley who boarded the train at Stafford. He was in civilian clothes and told her he was a Flight Sergeant Pilot.

In his London hotel possibly the 'City of Quebec', Leckey chummed up with some American airmen and by sheer chance, one American recognised Leckey as the man whose photograph had been circulated as wanted for murder in the national press. He immediately informed Marylebone Police Station and shortly afterwards Leckey, who had by then stolen several well filled American wallets, was arrested by Constable Riggs. He was arrested, taken to Marylebone Station where some time later, he was handed over to Detective Superintendent Smeed and Detective Inspector Pierce of Folkestone. Once there, he was formally charged with the murder and rape of Caroline Trayler.

The post mortem examination of the body revealed that she had been savagely strangled and raped: forensic evidence at his trial revealed that dark hairs which were found on the uniform Leckey was wearing on the night of the murder (he had left his uniform at his home) were identical with the hair of the unfortunate girl. Fibres from his khaki shirt matched the minute strands found under Caroline's fingernails.

Gunner Leckey appeared before Judge Singleton at the Old Bailey on 21st September of that year and right through his trial refused to say a word apart from agreeing that his name was that on the charge sheet and pleading not guilty. Even though he remained silent, probably because he was told to do so, the evidence

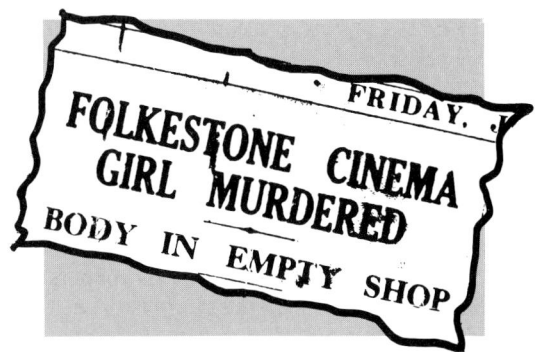

Left: Caroline Ellen Trayler

Below: The scene of the crime

against him, particularly the forensic evidence, was overwhelming, also the fact that his mate Bombardier Knight had seen him leave the public house with Caroline, was a vital point. The theft of the paybooks and cash also assisted the Prosecution Counsel - Mr Flower. Defending Counsel was Mr J. Casswell. After all the witnesses had been heard, and pleas submitted by the two Counsels. Mr Justice Singleton made his summing up and addressed the jury. He included: "If Leckey left the girl as he said at 10.30 p.m. (this was in the only statement made by Leckey) why did he not return to camp on the transport provided? It was still daylight". It was then he uttered the words that would free Leckey who was guilty as sin, as the evidence proved. He said; "This man is always so cool and collected, his actions are not those of an innocent man. Throughout his trial he has remained silent and from that there is only one inference you can draw."

The jury retired with the parting remarks of the judge ringing in their ears. They were out for only half an hour before returning and announcing a verdict of 'guilty'. Leckey was sentenced to death by hanging in the time honoured manner.

Even before he returned to prison, his Counsel was preparing his grounds for appeal against the verdict based on the judge's summing up of course. When this appeal was heard by the Court of Appeal, it was stressed that the fact that Leckey remained silent was not relevant to the issue as it would have been had not Mr Justice Singleton made that fatal error in his summing up which literally saved Gunner Leckey from hanging. For in early November 1943, Leckey's appeal succeeded - it had to - and once again he became a free man, but one with the cruel murder and rape of a young girl on his conscience.

According to newspaper reports, Sergeant Trayler in North Africa knew nothing of his wife's murder until he read about the case when he was a patient in a desert hospital. That was on July 20th. His appeal for compassionate leave was refused and he was officially informed of his wife's death in early September. No reasons for this unforgiveable delay have ever been released and the Ministry of Defence refuse to give any information to anyone other than a relative - if any remain. There is no doubt that after such callous treatment, Edgar Trayler took the decision to desert from his Unit in the North African campaign. Just how he managed to get back to this country on a journey that took almost six weeks has never been disclosed. Did he I wonder travel through enemy occupied territory or was it through a neutral country?

On November 7th, 1943, he visited his in-laws in Folkestone but whether he was under Army escort is not known. I could find no further mention of Edgar Trayler in local newspapers, the big dailys or in the 'Soldier' magazine in which I appealed for information about him last year. A Durham based newspaper could not help, neither could the Durham Light Infantry Museum, or even the Army Museum. I have formed the opinion that someone somewhere is covering up; I wonder why. The omnipotent M.O.D. can tell us but refuse to disclose any information to anyone other than a relative. I can find no trace of relatives on either side of the Traylers. They are either dead or moved away from the area, it seems.

Mr and Mrs Stapleton are both dead and the present occupants of 3, Sussex Road, know nothing about the tragic case. Ironically, it is conceivably possible that ex Gunner Leckey is still alive somewhere in this country, but he I feel sure will never come forward. If Edgar Trayler is still alive, only he can really enlighten us as to how he managed to get back to this country, I cannot possibly envisage any M.O.D. pedagogue volunteering the information we require and that wall of silence remains unbroken.

If Leckey had not suddenly absented himself from the camp, it was quite likely that he would have not come under suspicion quite so quickly if at all.

The Crimes and Punishments of Knatchbull, Meredith and Mann

I have no doubt that every historian who is acquainted with the harsh regimes and punishments of the past, is fully aware that in 1718, the Government of George I introduced what transpired to be an extremely cruel form of punishment; I refer of course to transportation. This was introduced to deal with the ever growing numbers of criminals petty or otherwise. The few prisons we had in Britain were always full, and the time came when such institutions could hold no more prisoners. For many years the punishment for stealing property valued at more than five shillings or theft accompanied by burglary, was death by hanging. Horse and sheep stealing came into this category as well.

The minimum period of transportation was seven years and those who had their death sentence commuted to transportation considered themselves very fortunate. Until the latter part of the 18th century, transport was confined to America and her colonies. However, the final destination of prisoners aboard transport ships, was left to the discretion of the Captain. Some unscrupulous Masters even sold the most able of their convicts to land owners in America or the Spanish Colonies. After the discovery of Australia and it's colonisation, the Government decreed that certain ports in Australia would become penal colonies. Consequently, penal settlements were established in Sydney, Perth, Brisbane and Hobart in Tasmania. To this list we can add Norfolk Island, many miles north east of Australia, and escape from there was virtually impossible. That agonizingly long sea voyage of eighteen weeks or more, ensured without doubt that on average at least a quarter of the convicts, male or female, would perish before reaching their destination. For most of that nightmarish journey, they were all manacled and chained and there was no segregation of the sexes. Conditions on board were truly horrendous, food was scarce or inedible, scurvy and other diseases were rife and this vile form of punishment continued for almost a century; during this time more than 165,000 convicts, including the 67,000 sent to Tasmania, were sent to this new found colony. It paid every convict ship Master, to keep as many of the prisoners alive as he could. On arrival in Australia, he was given a bonus of £50, which was reduced if too many prisoners died envoyage. The ship's doctor fared even better, receiving half a guinea for each convict who landed in fairly good health.

One of those transported in 1824, for the theft of two guineas, was John Knatchbull. He was a serving naval officer and his parents were Baron Knatchbull and Fanny Knight, niece of Jane Austen. They reared ten children and John Knatchbull was, without doubt, the proverbial black sheep although he had been well educated, having attended the Grammar School at Ashford in Kent.

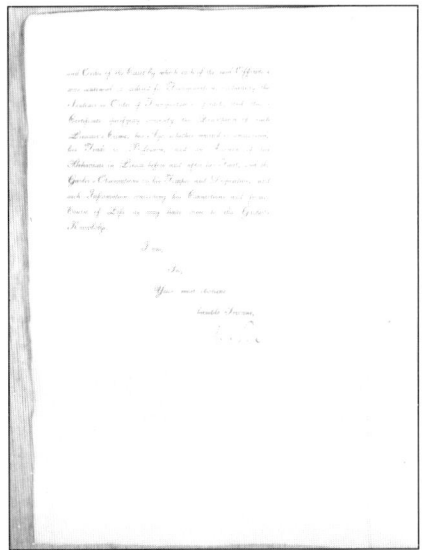 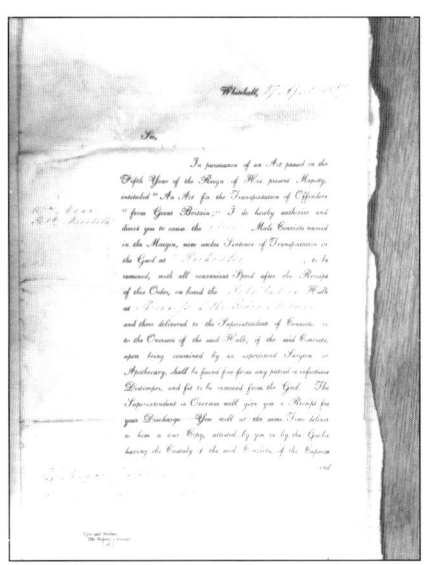

This is the authorisation from the Home Office directing the Governor of Rochester Gaol to deliver the two men to the prison hulk 'Retribution' before transferring to a convict transport ship in the Medway

Knatchbull was a very plausible rogue and indeed earned a niche for himself in the history of Australia. In 1832, Knatchbull serving a term of fourteen years, was sentenced to death for forgery; he managed to talk his way out of this trip to the gallows by having it commuted to another seven years hard labour on Norfolk Island. Even then, he wasn't finished and with thirteen other convicts he hatched a plot to poison all the guards, steal a ship and sail to South America. This plot failed as someone informed the guard Commander. Knatchbull escaped death once again and his thirteen conspirators were duly hanged. Just why Knatchbull did not suffer the same fate is not explained in any of the appropriate books I studied.

However, he was it seems living on borrowed time, for on returning to Sydney as a ticket of leave man, he fell in love with a woman much younger than his 56 years. To impress the girl and also support her, he murdered Ellen Jamieson, a widow who ran a small shop in Darlinghurst Sydney. He was soon traced and caught and on 13th February, 1844, he was hanged. His plausibility and eloquence failed to make any impression on this occasion and so this ancestor of Lord Brabourne, paid the supreme penalty.

Included in the thousands of criminals who were transported from Kent in 1827, were Patrick Meredith and William Mann, both in their early twenties. Both had committed the crime of larceny; Meredith had stolen property belonging to a fellow guest at the Cock Inn Eastgate, near Rochester and was caught in the act. William Mann, a serving soldier stationed at Fort Pitt on the outskirts of the town,

Receipt for the two men signed by the overseer of the hulk

contrived to sneak into the hallowed precincts of the Officers Mess and stole two silver spoons valued at sixteen shillings. Unluckily for him, he was seen by the Mess Steward who promptly informed the Sergeant of the Guard. He in turn, alerted the Parade Sergeant Major who acting with commendable speed, organised a posse and scoured the Chatham streets for the miscreant. In less than an hour, they found him sauntering along the red light district of the Brook, having already sold one of the spoons.

Consequently, both men who were unknown to each other appeared before the Recorder at Rochester Quarter Sessions on April 24th 1827, and here they both received sentences of seven years transportation. Accordingly, an Official Order from the Home Office was sent to the Governor of Rochester Gaol, directing him to send the luckless pair to the prison hulk 'Retribution' anchored in Medway with several other dreary looking vessels. The document stated that the Apothecary on board must examine them to ensure they were not suffering from distemper or any putrid form of infection. Unfortunately, I could find no further mention of either but it is safe to assume, they were certified fit to travel the twelve thousand miles to what was generally thought to be a living hell on the other side of the world. Along with another two hundred miserable lice ridden prisoners, they were kept below decks in a stinking unlit hold chained and manacled for most of that nightmarish eighteen week journey. It is possible that both men were aware that at least twenty of their comrades including a proportion of females would never live to gaze on Botany Bay for the first time.

Although history tells what happened to Knatchbull, the respective fates of Meredith and Mann have yet to come to light. They could have been despatched to the notorious Port Arthur penal settlement in Tasmania, where in fact more than 67,000 convicts were landed during those unrelenting years. It was still called Van Diemen's Land at that time and the conditions prevailing in the Colony remained horrendous for many years. It was virtually impossible to escape and the foolish ones who tried were soon caught and hanged immediately. Today, it is generally known that a very large slice of Australia's sixteen million population, are direct descendants of those convicts; in fact many Australians are very proud of their backgrounds. On this theme, it is interesting to speculate on just how many present day Australian's ancestors were conceived in the stench and darkness of those convict ship's holds. Segregation was eventually introduced about the middle of the 19th century and understandably, this move proved to be distinctly unpopular with both sexes in the voyages that followed.

In conclusion, it is interesting to concede that today, we can fly to Australia in less than 24 hours, compared to the three to four months journey cooped up in one of those grimly forbidding convict ships of the last century.

The Murder of Constable Baxter at Chatham

In a country now wallowing in ever increasing violence, crime, greed and corruption in all walks of life, the Kent County Constabulary, founded in 1857 under the command of ex Army Captain Ruxton, the very first Chief Constable, has a really remarkable record; only two policemen have been murdered since its historical inception. But this in no way implies that there have not been numerous attempts to slaughter or maim our policemen. Vicious assaults on police officers have soared to an all time high throughout the County. As far back as 1960, especially at Sheerness, where I was serving, assaults on police were commonplace.

However, I am writing about murder and the first of the two cases was that of P.C. Israel May at Snodland on 27th August, 1873. He was found lying in a pool of blood, battered to death with his own truncheon. It was abundantly clear that a violent struggle had taken place where the body was found and the first piece of evidence was a bloodstained cap and shortly afterwards, a severed pair of braces. It was soon established that these articles belonged to Thomas Atkins, a local labourer; a search was instigated immediately and six days later, Atkins was arrested at Kingsdown. Although he confessed to the murder, he insisted that the first blow had been struck by the constable, who hit Atkins on the head with his truncheon. In his defence, Atkins declared that he certainly would not have attacked the constable otherwise. Significantly, he was not asked just why he launched such a murderous attack.

At the trial, several witnesses included in their statements the fact that the previous night Israel May had made several attempts to rouse Atkins from a drunken stupor and following this, Atkins had threatened violence. During the proceedings at the Assize Court, it was disclosed (and it would not be allowed today) that the father of Atkins was found guilty of murdering his wife many years before and had been adjudged insane. As for Thomas Atkins, he was extremely fortunate that the gullible jury were mercifully disposed and returned a verdict of manslaughter. Eventually he served 15 years of his twenty year sentence and then emigrated to America. The Chief Constable and sixty members of the Force (almost a quarter) attended Israel's funeral. But, symbolic of those hard times, his widow with three young children, was awarded the meagre sum of £63 17s 6d; this was equal to one year's pay for Israel. Today, she would receive many thousands of pounds.

Almost eighty years later on 4th June 1951, Police Constable Alan Baxter, was mown down by a hail of bullets from a Sten gun fired by a Chatham youth called Alan Derek Poole, in an isolated country lane near Luton just outside Chatham. Alan Baxter died in hospital later the following day. On the night of the murder,

Poole, a deserter from the Royal Corps of Signals, had been seen by witnesses carrying the Sten gun in the Luton area. He was wearing a mask and fired a warning shot in the direction of the thoroughly scared witnesses who immediately, and justifiably, scampered for cover. But why they waited an hour before strolling into Chatham Police Station to report the incident, instead of using the 999 emergency telephone system, remains a mystery. Another query I asked myself, was based on the fact that only a Sergeant and two constables, all unarmed, were despatched to the area in an ancient police van. WHY? Should not additional patrols have been sent to the scene along with a marksman as a back up team? I concede that the radio communication system was in its embryonic stage, but it functioned well enough. To the best of my knowledge, this has never been explained. The Kent Force even had a trained dog in 1951, but it was never brought in. Arriving at the scene where Poole was last spotted, Sergeant Langford circled the shed indicated by one of the youthful witnesses as Poole's hiding place at the far side of a meadow. Leaving P.C. Brown at the edge of the meadow, and Alan Baxter in the van, parked in the lane, presumably to monitor the situation and report by radio accordingly to Operations Room. Cautiously, Langford made a circuit of the shed and then peered through a broken window; his eyes focussed on Poole and two young females. As the Sergeant doubled round the shed to intercept the trio, which was a very foolish act and extremely inadvisable, the gunman fired single shots at him. This prompted Langford and his witness to dive for cover. In common with most automatic weapons, the Sten gun was capable of firing both single shots or a continuous burst of fire. After leaving the shed, it appears that Poole and the two girls ran across the field to where the police van was parked. Shortly afterwards, a number of shots were heard coming from the van's position. When Sergeant Langford reached the van, Poole and the girls had disappeared and P.C. Baxter was lying crumpled in the road bleeding profusely from a number of gunshot wounds.

For some unaccountable reason, the van's radio was not working and Sergeant Langford's first priority was to get the seriously injured constable to hospital. Placing the now unconscious form of Alan Baxter in the rear of the van, he drove off to St Bartholomews Hospital with all haste. At that time, I was one of a score of probationer constables enduring what was then termed a refresher course at Force Headquarters, Maidstone. It was 3 a.m. on 5th June, when we were roused from slumber by a loud banging of doors in our sleeping quarters and we were given five minutes to get dressed and muster on the parade ground. We were then rushed to Chatham by car and this hair raising journey took no longer than twenty minutes - it could have been even less. On arrival at Chatham Police Station we were briefed and told just what was expected of us. It was during that grey transitional period which heralds the dawn, when tingling with excitement and, yes, a little apprehension, we commenced a wide scale search of the country area in the vicinity of Luton and other likely places. Our only weapons were our truncheons, although the Deputy Chief Constable, bringing up the rear, had managed to acquire a revolver. Later I discovered that more than one hundred

Left: Murder weapon held by CID man

Above: The funeral, at Charing Crematorium, of PC Baxter. He was shot by Alan Derek Poole

Right: CID man in Poole's dug-out hide away. Note the depth

policemen and servicemen took part in that search. At 7 a.m. the two girls who had accompanied Poole the night before, both Approved School abscondees, confirmed the identity of Poole; they left him some time after the shooting. At the same time, the Criminal Records Office at Force Headquarters released the news that Poole had a criminal record which commenced when he was a juvenile. His brother too had such a record. The military authorities had also circulated his description as a deserter. During that long exhausting search through dark woods, dew drenched fields and deserted buildings, we found one of Poole's primitive hideouts on the fringe of a wood.

Looking back, I realise that because of the lack of communications we were all blissfully unaware that as we were searching the countryside, Poole had slunk back into his Council owned home in Symonds Avenue at Chatham. Eventually, a cordon of Police, some armed by now, had surrounded the house and about 9 a.m. a burst of gunfire from an upstairs bedroom, was directed at police officers on waste ground at the back of the house. Quite rightly, the fire was returned and tear gas grenades were fired into the house. At 10.45 a.m. Chief Constable Ferguson ordered a direct assault on the house. Upstairs in his bedroom, Poole was lying dead with his loaded Sten gun resting across his body. The post mortem examination revealed that the police marksman's bullet entered his left side and punctured both lungs. This vicious young killer was alone in the house.

A search of the house revealed a trap hatch in the floor of the sitting room, with enough space beneath to enable a man to hide. In the back garden was another large hole, at the entrance to a tunnel leading back to the house. Had Poole lived long enough to complete the tunnel, electric lighting would have been installed. It was abundantly clear that the killer's parents had actively connived in the excavation of this tunnel; no action was taken against them. At the inquest on P.C. Baxter's death, there was only one possible verdict - murdered by Poole. The death of the murderer was deemed to be justifiable homicide.

So ended one of the biggest manhunts in the history of the Kent Police. For some time afterwards however, I was still pondering on the fact that even after Poole's death, many coppers engaged in the search were still engaged in the hunt by stopping and searching cars and buses in the Medway area. It would have been quite simple and perfectly logical for a motor cyclist to speed out to the searchers and pass on the good news. The lack of radio communication could not be blamed for this appalling lapse. If this had occurred today, a top level investigation would have been launched immediately. Fortunately, the Police and the necessary technology have vastly improved since 1951 and it is to be hoped that the number of murdered Kent coppers will remain at two.

The Death of the Battleship 'Bulwark' in 1914

The flat, featureless and undulating stretch of coastline between Sheerness and Chatham was shrouded in a veil of murky grey mist in the early hours of Thursday 26th November, 1914. This mist did not, however, hide from view the majestic sight of several of our capital ships belonging to the British Grand Fleet which were moored to buoys in the Medway in line ahead. The Great War commenced some time before this and both sides had lost more ships than they expected so early in the conflict. In addition, the German Army was advancing on a wide front in Belgium and the Allies were retreating. The squadron of battleships, cruisers and destroyers, were just a part of the Grand Fleet and included such veterans as the 'Lord Nelson' Admiral Burney's flagship, the Formidable, Irresistible, Venerable, Implacable and the fifteen thousand ton battleship, 'Bulwark'... She was built in 1899 at the cost of one million pounds, was 430 feet in length with a beam of 75 feet, less than half the size of the battleships of later years. Her armaments included four 12 inch guns, two batteries of six inch and a number of smaller weapons and four torpedo tubes.

Her freeboard from bow to stern was protected by a layer of nine inch thick steel, which tapered to six inches at her bow and stern. Like her sister ships, she was a coal burner and carried 2,000 tons of coal and was capable of steaming at eighteen knots. She was first commissioned in 1902 spending the first five years of her existence in the Mediterranean. From 1907 until 1908, the Bulwark was the flagship of the Nore, commanded by Captain Robert Falcon Scott, a man destined to die in the icy wastes of the South Pole a few years later. On the fateful morning of the 26th November, she was commanded by Captain Guy Sclater, who joined the ship in November the year before. His ship's company comprised 780 officers and men and on that historical morning, they were all on board. The ship was moored to No.17 Buoy in Kethole Reach between Sheerness and Chatham and within sight of the aptly named Dead Man's Island. The whole Fleet was protected from submarine attack by a system of booms and wire nets stretched across the estuary. Coaling ship had taken place the day before consequently, the ship had been washed down and virtually free of coal dust. Breakfast was taken at the usual time of 07.30 and the cooks of each mess were busy clearing away the breakfast crockery and in some cases preparing the midday meals. In those harsh days, they were prepared for cooking by the men living in each mess on a rota basis. The food was then taken to the galley for cooking. Some of the crew were making their way to their places of work whilst a few still lingered on the mess deck drinking tea from china basins; there were no breakfast cups at that time. One such imbiber was Able Seaman Stephen Marshall and, in his cabin at the stern, Captain Sclater was enjoying his tea in more luxurious surroundings. On the fo'c'sle, between the capstans, the Royal Marine Band were playing some stirring tunes as was the custom. In fact some Captains encouraged their men to double around the upper deck in time with the music for ten minutes or so.

In other words everything aboard the Bulwark was going according to plan as usual on a normal working day. One of the men serving in the Bulwark was my 17 year old uncle, Harry Bishop, who had just graduated to the rank of Ordinary Seaman having joined as a Boy Seaman two years before at a weekly wage of five shillings. Providentially, he was never to know that at 07.50 he would be blown to eternity leaving just fourteen survivors. According to A. B. Marshall, who was one of the lucky fourteen, he was still drinking his tea when he felt what he called a colossal draught and found himself soaring way above the mainmast, which was then engulfed in a sheet of crimson flame. He never discovered just how he came to be airborne in this manner and there was not the slightest warning of the impending disaster. Marshall recalled how he felt the heat of the searing flames and at the same time heard a thunderous roar coming from the bowels of the ship. As he splashed into the icy waters of the Medway, another frightening roar arose from the innards of the Bulwark. By that time he was swimming and realising his tea basin had crunched into his face, cutting both cheeks, he soon discarded the utensil.

The echoes of both explosions occurred repeatedly with an eerie repetition. The explosions were heard as far away as Chatham and Rainham and in Sheerness many windows were shattered and hundreds of spectators rushed to the seafront. Able Seaman Spakeman found himself in the water spinning like a top; he too had not the faintest idea of how he was levitated and thrown overboard by the first of the two almighty explosions. Leading Seaman Johnson was yet another who was catapulted into the river and described the explosions and the sheets of flame that engulfed the Bulwark as a bloody nightmare which he would never forget. Automatically, he grabbed a large cylindrical oil covered object by his side and found it to be a torpedo. On board the Implacable, the nearest ship to the Bulwark, Midshipman Arthur Wellesley Clark was standing on the compass platform with some of his fellow snotties, as they were affectionately known, awaiting the arrival of the bearded Chief Bunting Tosser (Signalman) who was putting them through their communication drills in semaphore and the morse code. As young Clark gazed astern at the Bulwark, a few hundred feet away, he found himself paralysed as in abject horror he saw a huge crimson sheet of flame erupt from the midship portion of the Bulwark and then heard the two devastating explosions which caused him to duck instinctively. Transfixed he watched the death throes of the mighty Bulwark as flames and huge columns of black smoke spewed from the dying battleship. He then saw the mainmast disappear and agonisingly watched the ship or what was left of her settle lower in the water. By then the Midshipman had discarded his semaphore flags and was scuttling towards the boat deck with his peers. They had all heard the terse command of "Away all boats" and needed

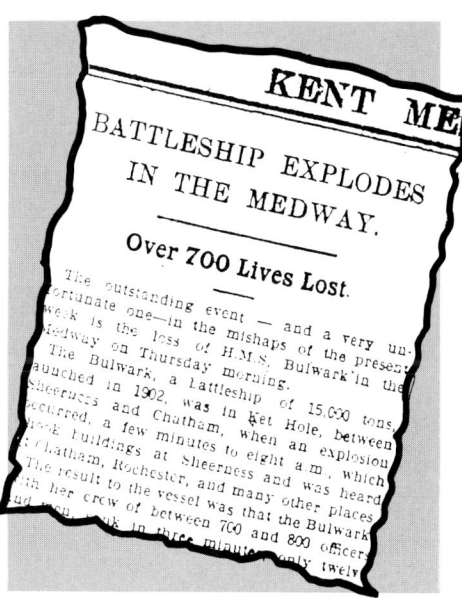

Above: Cutting from Local Newspaper

Left: Ordinary Seaman Harry Bishop 1914

HMS Bulwark, Battleship, 15,000 tons

no prompting. Even as he ran, this incredible phenomena caused the Implacable to rock violently as she lay moored to her buoy.

At first it was thought, and justifiably so, that a submarine had penetrated the defences and fired torpedoes, this was later discarded. Exactly the same drill was being performed aboard the battleship Irresistible and within minutes a flotilla of small boats was heading towards the now empty berth of the Bulwark. She had completely disappeared. Even as the rescue boats sped to the scene, dense showers of debris and dust were falling on and around them. Terribly mutilated bodies were hurled for thousands of yards around the Fleet. Captain Sclater's ceremonial frock coat with the gold lace on the sleeves but still recognisable was just one of the articles picked up by Midshipman Clark's pinnace. Also retrieved were hammocks, ditty boxes and chests of drawers from officers cabins; Official documents and letters floated past and picked up; One letter written by a man to his wife read; "I am longing to see you again." A poignant, touching wish that would never come true. The few that survived were taken back to one of the other ships sick bays as soon as possible. Many others survived for a short while but later succumbed to their terrible injuries. Leading Seaman Johnson's body was badly bruised caused by his contact with the water from a great height.

Ironically, some of the bodies and even parts of limbs were found on the mud flats surrounding Dead Mans Island, the graveyard of many a French sailor and indeed convicts in later years. One body taken from the water was that of Captain Morton, the Officer commanding the Royal Marine Detachment. He and Surgeon Commander Nix were the only two who were readily identified. In all 28 bodies were recovered, most of them utterly unrecognisable.

That same day, the First Lord of the Admiralty, Winston Churchill, solemnly announced the loss of the Bulwark to a shocked Parliament and at the same time announced that a Court of Enquiry would be set up as soon as possible. Churchill was never forgiven for his obscene haste in instigating that enquiry which in fact was held the very next day. Churchill explained to the House that the battleship Bulwark blew up that morning at her moorings with tragically a heavy loss of life. The senior officers present are convinced that there was an internal magazine explosion which rent the ship asunder. Then he added; "An enquiry will be held tomorrow which possibly may throw more light on this occurrence, but I deeply regret to say that between 700 and 800 men perished".

Next day the Press, local and national, reported the tragedy at great length. The correspondent of one paper picked up the story of a mysterious stranger who had joined the Sheerness onlookers, to gaze triumphantly at the scene of the disaster, before hurrying away. This story was given considerable prominence and the Germans jubilantly claimed that one of their submarines had sunk the Bulwark. After the Inquest held at the Royal Naval Hospital, Chatham, on the bodies which had so far been recovered, 21 of the victims were buried in Woodland Cemetery at Gillingham with full naval honours.

In the middle of December, a brief report of the findings of the Court of Enquiry was issued. It said little that was useful and indeed made one unjustified assumption: "It is clear from the evidence produced" ran the official statement, "that the explosion which caused the loss of the ship was due to the accidental ignition of ammunition on board. There is no evidence to support a suggestion that the explosion was caused by treachery on board the Bulwark or to enemy action." This Court of Enquiry concluded that it was most likely that the uncovered charges of cordite, which were in contact with the hot bulkhead had somehow ignited and detonated one of the 275 x 6 inch shells which should not have been stored anywhere near the cordite contrary to naval gunnery regulations. So ended one of the greatest naval disasters of the Great War and the probable cause of this tragedy will not it seems, ever be known.

By some strange coincidence and quirk of fate, almost exactly the same events occurred aboard the cruiser 'Natal' on Thursday December 30th, 1915. On this occasion, the ship was anchored in Cromarty Firth and amongst the 360 killed were several naval wives and nurses from the hospital ship 'Plassey' moored a few hundred yards away. The women had been invited to a party aboard the 'Natal'. Again, the actual cause of the massive explosion which capsized and destroyed the cruiser was never determined although the theory of an explosion in the magazine was probably correct. On reading the account of this enormous tragedy, my sympathies for the four leave breakers who were locked in the forward cells, were most profound. It seems that the Corporal of Marines who had the cell keys, was killed as he was making his way to the cell block to release those unfortunate men who died such an agonisingly slow death as their ship slowly capsized and sank. Many sailors from Kent were aboard that ill fated ship which took just five minutes after the explosion to roll over, capsize and sink.

A Bent Copper of the Last Century

When the Kent County Constabulary was formed in 1857, under the command of John Henry Ruxton, a retired Army Captain, prospects of promotion were extremely limited. Only the brightest and best educated had any chance of rising above the rank of constable - and only then if they took good care to avoid falling foul of the feared Ruxton. George English was one of the few who made it to Superintendent. After a few years as superintending constable (he had the ability of being able to read and write), he was promoted to Superintendent under the provisions of the 1839 legislation. His weekly wage rose to about £2.14 shillings, three times that of a constable. But this was not enough for English; on March 20th 1870, as Officer in Charge of Ashford Police Station, he stole or embezzled the sum of £250 in sovereigns and silver, which had been found in the home of Mrs Mary James, by Sergeant Marsh and Constable Hollands. These two officers had been directed to search the house after Mrs James had been arrested for larceny from a clothes line the previous day.

The stolen clothes were found close to a box containing the hoard of coins. A quantity of property stolen from Ashford Railway Station was also confiscated. In accordance with the Chief Constable's Standing Orders, the property and the coins were handed to Supt. English. A receipt was given to Mrs James before she was put in a cell. She was never charged with the theft of the money and in any case she stoutly maintained that it belonged to her. English, then 40, was considerably attracted by what in those days was a very large sum of money and he made up his mind to have some or all of it. He started by chatting up Mrs James as she languished in her dark cell. English lived in the flat over the Station with his wife and children. He asked Mrs James, whose husband had left her, to begin a new life with him in far off Australia; the cost of the fares coming out of the £250 of course. But Mrs James was no fool, well not in that respect, and refused his offer. She gave him the brush off again when he was foolish enough to visit her in Canterbury Prison. This was strictly forbidden in any case. But English was not one to give in easily. Very soon, he tagged on to Mrs Polly Wilson, another Ashford woman; she fell for his patter and agreed to travel with him to Australia. She had no money for the fare in any case. The crafty Supt. English, in one last attempt to persuade Mrs James, paid a solicitor the sum of £10 to conduct her defence. No doubt this money came from the stolen £250 belonging to Mrs James.

Ruxton suspected nothing when English asked him for a period of extended leave to enable him to visit a sick relative. This gave him time to shop around shipping agents in the London area and eventually he booked passages for himself, Polly Wilson and for some unexplained reason, the errant husband of Mrs James.

Chief Constable John Henry Ruxton, 1857-1870

Just where he fitted in remains a mystery. Neither Mrs English nor anyone else knew of the Superintendent's intentions and on Monday 29 August 1870, the Beatrice sailed from London to arrive in Moreton Bay, Brisbane, on January 11th the following year. When Chief Constable Ruxton heard about the escapade of English, and the theft of the cash, he ordered enquiries, which led to the discovery of English's destination and his companion.

The angry Chief Constable immediately sent a young constable, Robert Breeze of Maidstone, to pursue and arrest English. Travelling overland to India, probably Calcutta, he boarded the first ship sailing to Brisbane. He had been given a limited amount of money and an arrest warrant, on what was probably the longest journey ever undertaken by a policeman to arrest a criminal. Definite confirmation of the whereabouts of English was telegraphed to Breeze when he arrived in India. In any case, he made much better time on his journey than the Beatrice in which English was sailing along with Mrs Wilson. And so it was that when the Beatrice anchored in Moreton Bay at Brisbane, on December 28th 1870, Constable Breeze who had been awaiting her arrival, hired a rowing boat to take him out to the ship. Dutifully, if not joyfully, he boarded the Beatrice and found George English lounging with Polly Wilson on the poop deck. In his evidence at the trail of English at Maidstone, in July, the following year, Breeze deposed, said the Maidstone Journal reporter; "I went up to him and asked him; 'Do you know

OLD "CLIPPER" RIVALRIES REVIVED: A TRANS-OCEAN RACE BY SAIL.

A View of the 4-masted Barque BEATRICE with all sails furled lying at Anchor in FALMOUTH Harbour

me sir?' 'No, I do not' replied the startled English, 'but I suspect you are a policeman sent to arrest me all the way from England'."

    Breeze then told Mr Justice Brown sitting with a Grand Jury of 21 Justices, that he accompanied English to his cabin where he formally arrested him and charged him with the embezzlement of the £250, and the theft of two gold watches, belonging to a Folkestone jeweller. When he was questioned about the missing money, English declared; "I have left that at home and I have witnesses to prove it". P.C. Breeze did not believe him of course and on searching the cabin, he found a box containing full and half sovereigns. English made a feeble attempt to explain that the money belonged to Mrs Wilson. Young Robert Breeze knew he had acquired sufficient evidence to arraign English before the Brisbane Magistrates, the following morning. After hearing the evidence, the magistrates remanded English (by then demoted by telegraph) to the custody of Constable Breeze. According to the Brisbane Courier of January 21st 1871, Breeze found the two gold watches and a gold chain in the cabin occupied by English and Polly Wilson.

    Constable Breeze was in a quandary when the realisation dawned on him that he had insufficient money to pay for the fare of English, which amounted to the sum of £25. His ship was due to sail on January 25th 1871, and Breeze had to apply to the Brisbane Central Authority for permission to extract that amount from the stolen money. It appears that Polly Wilson remained in Brisbane being unable to pay her fare, and Breeze and English arrived back in England on March 24th 1871. After a brief appearance before the Maidstone Magistrates, charged with the embezzlement and the theft of the gold watches and chain, English appeared before the Assize Court on July 24th the same year; he was also charged with obtaining an additional £107 from the luckless Mrs James. The cunning English had told the gullible Mrs James that the £107 she had in a Trustee Savings account at Rye, would be confiscated as part of her punishment. "It will be that much safer with me, my dear" he assured Mrs James. The unsuspecting woman meekly signed the money over to English and also entrusted all her goods and chattels to the rascal. Being unable to write, she made her mark on the document drawn up by English.

When Chief Constable Ruxton was called to give evidence regarding the antecedent history of the one time Superintendent, he told the Court rather pompously; "English had acted in a false manner as long ago as 1862, when he appropriated a gold pin owned by Captain Wallace of Shorncliffe Barracks. Prior to this, the pin had been stolen by a petty thief." English strongly denied the offence stating that he had been given the pin by another officer who had died recently (very conveniently). Strangely enough Ruxton did not offer an explanation as to why no action had been taken against English at the time. Ruxton went on to describe the theft of a dinghy by English, which had been washed ashore and possessed by the Customs and Excise men. The boat had been handed to the police at Folkestone as found property and it was kept at Sandgate for some more than a year, before the greedy George English who was temporarily stationed at Folkestone sold it for £8. Ruxton pointed out that English had no authority to dispose of the boat, but once again he failed to outline just what action, if any, he had taken against English. I have a suspicion that both were Freemasons, it certainly has all the hallmarks. However, Ruxton when concluding his evidence said "The conduct of English was most injurious to the Force and indeed to the whole country. The Police could not now apprehend a prisoner without being taunted by members of the public regarding the conduct of English".

English was found not guilty on the charge of embezzlement, which I found rather surprising as did Judge Blackburn. The jury found the prisoner guilty of the thefts of the two watches and Judge Blackburn made his views known in no uncertain manner. He addressed English as follows; "I shall consider you guilty of the offence of embezzlement, as I am utterly incapable of comprehending how the jury came to throw out the charge. Now having heard your past record, they must know that they found a verdict directly in the teeth of the evidence and the facts. I therefore pass on to you a sentence of seven years penal servitude". Incredibly English served only two years of his sentence, no explanation appears to have been given for this act of leniency. On his release, he moved to London where he worked as a carpenter. In 1878, he had the gall to write to Ruxton requesting the return of the money found in his cabin by P.C. Breeze. Ruxton had to refuse of course. As for the luckless Mrs James, the true owner of the cash, even though she probably came across it dishonestly, her repeated pleas for restitution went unheeded and she died in very poor circumstances a few years later. Even now, it would be very interesting to know just where that balance of £250 was deposited. There is certainly no sign of it in Ashford Police Station today.

Chief Constable Ruxton was not the paragon of virtue that some senior officers of the past would have us believe. For instance, he had the audacity to let it be known that Sergeant Marsh and Constable Hollands were mainly to blame for the downfall of George English. He had the two officers brought before him and delivered a withering and vitriolic reprimand. He told them they should have entered in their notebooks, the full details of all the events leading up to the handing over of the money to English. This was sheer unadulterated eyewash which was in my opinion connected to the fact that Ruxton and English were Freemasons. Marsh and Hollands were so incensed by this blatant injustice, that they resigned from the Kent Constabulary.

It is to be hoped that today, in Kent's modern Police Force, such nefarious officers as English will not be found.

Battle of the Dover Straits

When the war in Europe ended in 1945, several books were written about the daring exploits of our coastal craft crews in the Straits of Dover and the North Sea. Those light coastal craft, as they were called, consisted of Motor Torpedo Boats (M.T.B.'s) Motor Gun Boats (M.G.B.'s) and Motor Launches (M.L.'s). There were also trawlers and tugs converted into minesweepers. When the war began, England could boast of just one flotilla of each type. They operated from Dover, Felixstowe - (H.M.S. Beehive) and Ramsgate - (H.M.S. Fervent). Folkestone was also used on occasions. Being pre-war vintage, our boats were not very reliable and in fact inadequate, apart from the torpedoes of our M.T.B.'s.

In 1940, with the threat of invasion looming ominously close with more than forty enemy Divisions and half a million men in occupied France, ready for the 'off', work was put in hand to expand the numbers of coastal craft until 1942, we had more than 200 and not before time. They were all built by such firms as Thornycroft, Vosper Fairmile, and the British Power Boat Company. When America entered the war in 1941, she sent across an ever increasing number of much larger and more efficient vessels which were far superior to our own craft. Not only were they superior in size, they were also much more heavily armoured. They had Oerlikons and rotating turrets of twin mounted 0.5 machine guns pointed menacingly from stem to stern.

Consequently, the larger boats were manned by crews of more than thirty in some cases and invariably they were piped to action stations immediately they left harbour at dusk. Their shallow draught enabled them to creep in dangerously close to the enemy shore and in time the Dover Strike Force, as it was eventually called, proved to be a formidable adversary. Some time later, there were several flotillas based in Dover, which predictably became the Headquarters of the Coastal Craft. Dover Harbour Station became the nerve centre and was aptly called H.M.S. Wasp. The first Commander in Chief was Commodore Cunliffe and he was soon followed by Admiral Sir Pridham-Wippell; he in turn was replaced by Admiral Sir Bertram Ramsay. The majority of the ship's crew were billeted in the Lord Arden Hotel, just a couple of hundred yards from the Station. Today, this building is known as Southern House and was once the Head Office of Sealink Ferry Company.

When I entered the portals of Southern House some time ago, I eagerly scanned the walls of the foyer and the staircase, fully expecting them to be literally plastered with photographs of the Strike Force craft and perhaps some of their brave crews; at least something to indicate to the visiting public, that the building played an important part in the battle of the narrow seas. Regrettably, I saw nothing of that nature and no mention of the courageous men who earned such

Royal Temple Yacht Club, with the blue verandah.

honours through their bravery as several D.S.O.'s and numerous D.S.C.'s and an equal number of lesser accolades, such as the D.S.M. and C.G.M.'s. Indeed, far too many of those medals were awarded posthumously.

Over at Ramsgate, several flotillas of M.G.B.'s and a small number of M.T.B.'s converted into minesweepers were based in the harbour. This Ramsgate base was known as H.M.S. Fervent and the Headquarters was situated in the old Victorian Harbour Railway Station. The Station was closed in 1926 and transformed into an Amusement Park. The two mile stretch of tunnel which terminated at Dumpton Park, was used for the storage of essential supplies and armaments and also sleeping quarters for some of the coastal craft crews. The commissioned officers were bedded down in the utopian splendour of the Royal Temple Yacht Club, overlooking the harbour. Today, a few of those wartime veterans still make the occasional and nostalgic visit to the Club, where they probably recall and recount those dark days of 1940 and afterwards, when they and the Dover based men were often alerted to rescue one of our pilots who had baled out over the Channel. Sometimes, the rescued pilot was one of the enemy. On one occasion, an M.T.B. sped to the rescue of a German pilot entangled in the voluminous folds of his parachute. Just as he was being hauled inboard, three low flying enemy seaplanes dived on the craft straddling her with savage bursts of machine gun fire. The skipper of the M.T.B. had no option but to zoom away at full speed.

Also based at Dover for most of the war years were flotillas manned by the Free French, the Dutch, Belgians and Polish. A very strange and amusing incident occurred to a Dutch manned M.T.B. which came across a German raft holding ten survivors from an 'E' Boat which had been destroyed by one of our M.T.B.'s. On

MTB in action

being taken aboard and placed below decks, they immediately assumed that their destination was Holland, when they observed a large portrait of Queen Wilhelmina on one of the bulkheads. What a shock they had when the boat purred smoothly into Wellington Dock at Dover.

When it was discovered that the enemy was laying mines in the Straits, including the deadly magnetic types, several of the old type M.T.B.'s were converted into minesweepers by having their torpedo tubes removed to be replaced by paravanes and their launching equipment. All the ships of the Dover Strike Force carried depth charges in addition to the torpedoes of the M.T.B.'s. Every skipper became an expert at nipping in between the convoy lines of enemy ships under cover of darkness, to catapult, eject or simply drop depth charges as close to the selected target as possible. Such tactics were decidedly hazardous of course and the crew knew it; there was always the possibility of being shot up at point blank range. However, it seemed that the success rate outweighed the dangers of retaliation from the enemy escorts or indeed from the merchant ships themselves.

For about two years the Ramsgate based M.G.B. Flotilla under the command of Lieutenant G. K. Richards D.S.O. D.S.C. were often in action. He earned his D.S.O. on the night of April 4th 1943, when, with great daring, he and his highly trained crew attacked and sank a large heavily armed enemy trawler. Proudly, they returned to Ramsgate with more than 20 prisoners. This happened just after he had sank an 'E' Boat and captured the survivors. Although even more successes were to follow his number was up on the night of 27th May, the same year, when he and his gallant crew were killed in action as they attacked a heavily escorted enemy convoy just off the coast of Dunkirk.

His place as Flotilla Leader was taken by another youthful and incredibly keen officer, Lieutenant Rooper, already the holder of the D.S.C. He too knew no fear as he demonstrated on the night of July 24th 1943, when he encountered two 'E' Boats in mid Channel. He sank one with a single torpedo, and the other badly damaged by his crews gunfire, sank shortly afterwards. Regrettably Lieutenant Rooper was killed on Christmas Eve of that year, when his ship attacked yet another very large and closely guarded convoy as it zig zagged through the Channel.

In this drastically shortened version of the never ending battle of the Dover Straits, it would be quite unforgivable to omit just a few details of that momentous and now legendary occasion when on the morning of February 12th 1942, the German ships Scharnhorst, Gneisau and Prinz Eugen, made their audacious dash through the Channel en route for Kiel, from the much bombed port of Brest. It was 11.15 a.m. when C. in C. at Dover despatched five of his M.T.B.'s in a desperate and supremely optimistic attempt to locate and hopefully sink or damage one of those three capital ships. It was hopeless right from the start, as the atrocious weather and extremely rough seas reduced the speed of all the ships to less than half. One M.T.B. had to limp back to Dover, the other four pressed on cherishing a faint hope of getting near enough to the leviathans to fire off their torpedoes. This faint hope soon petered out when the escorting destroyers laid down a dense curtain of smoke. This action enabled the trio to veer sharply to starboard out of harm's way.

And yet those indescribably courageous pilots of the five Swordfish planes still penetrated that impregnable wall of smoke. One by one they were blasted out of existence and today this heroic episode is now writ large on our pages of wartime history.

Another very successful member of the Dover Strike Force and the skipper of an M.G.B. was Lieutenant Gould D.S.O. D.S.C. On the occasion when the German ships were sighted, he was ashore on official business when the news was rushed to him. Although he rushed back to his ship, it was too late to take an active part in the hunt. When he reluctantly realised the futility of his mission, he made his way back to base. However, there was some consolation as his gunners were sufficiently inspired to shoot down two Heinkels, and soon afterwards his crew rescued two of those brave Swordfish pilots.

There is no doubt that Lieutenant Gould was held in high esteem by his men, many of whom were seriously injured during encounters with enemy ships. In November 1941, he battled with 'E' Boats on two occasions and in the second clash, his vessel was badly damaged and caught fire. On board at the time was an old friend of mine, Able Seaman Reg Farbrace, who joined the Navy at the same time as I joined the Royal Marines. Reg sustained severe burns and spent a long time in East Grinstead Hospital. On the night of July, 24th 1943, Lt. Gould's craft ran into heavy and devastating gunfire from an enemy coastal craft. Gould retaliated immediately, but during this vicious exchange, Able Seaman Lanfear,

Plaque hanging in the Royal Temple Yacht Club

one of the gunners and a native of Broadstairs, suffered terrible injuries. Despite his wounds, he remained at his gun until collapsing through loss of blood. For this incredible display of guts, he was awarded the Conspicuous Gallantry Medal.

To relate in detail the numerous acts of heroism by the officers and men of our Light Coastal Craft, would be a truly mammoth task, however I would like to mention just a few more of the Coastal Craft Commanders, all of whom found a justifiable niche in naval history. The late Captain Peter Dickens, then a Lieutenant Commander, and a great grandson of the world renowned novelist, was one of our most successful commanders from 1942 onwards although in the main he operated from Felixstowe. His decorations included the D.S.O., D.S.C., M.B.E. and many Mentions in Despatches. Another such stalwart was the late Sir Peter Scott, who commanded an M.G.B. aptly named the Grey Goose. He too received several decorations for bravery and in his book entitled the Battle of the Narrow Seas, he was generous in his praise of Captain Dickens, Lt. Commander Hichen, Lt. Commander Bradford and Lieutenants Sidebottom and Lloyd. They all enjoyed, if that is the word, tremendous success in a number of lively actions.

For instance, when Lloyd came across four enemy flak ships, he torpedoed and sank one and turned his full fire power on to the other vessels, which fled in utter panic and confusion. A few days later, in that eventful week of 1942, he was patrolling dangerously close to the French coast when suddenly twin searchlight beams stabbed the darkness before focussing on his craft and a signalling lamp from the shore battery asked him to identify himself. The cheeky young Lieutenant ordered his signalman to flash back; "Hail Churchill". Simultaneously he ordered "full speed and let's get out of here". Before his ship was swallowed up in the darkness, several salvos of high explosives straddled his vessel.

Four MTB's converted to Minesweepers moored at Ramsgate. A depth charge is visible on the stern of the first

Our light coastal craft continued to seek out and destroy enemy shipping in 'Coffin Alley' as the Germans called the Straits, and also in the North Sea. They were of course busily engaged in that historic landing on the French coast on 'D' Day 1944. Today, it is generally accepted that Kent suffered much more than any other county during that holocaust and rightly earned the title of Front Line County and Dover became known as Hellfire Corner.

Regarding the name 'E' Boat, this is believed to be an abbreviation of Enemy War Motor Boat. This phrase was of course coined by the Royal Navy. Paravanes were made of steel about eight feet long and five feet wide, including their stubby projections shaped like the wings of a plane and adding stability. A cutting device was attached to the leading edge of each wing, which cut the mooring wires of floating mines just below the surface. Paravanes were streamed (towed) from the fo'c'sle on both sides at an angle of about thirty degrees and a hundred yards away from the ship.

The Manston Massacre, August 24th, 1955

About 10.45 a.m. on Wednesday, 24th August 1955, astonished holiday makers relaxing on Broadstairs centuries old pier, witnessed the start of a gun battle in which a 22 year old American airman died. The alarming events leading up to the shoot-out started at Manston Aerodrome about two hours before, when a coloured serviceman - Napoleon Green went totally berserk and ruthlessly slaughtered three of his comrades. Seven others, including two women were wounded in that ninety minutes of mayhem on that tranquil August day. Being in possession of an automatic .30 carbine and a revolver ensured that Green held a distinct advantage over anyone who dared challenge him.

Green belonged to a large American Air Force unit which had been stationed at Manston for several years; many of the men rented or even owned properties in the Thanet area. It seems that Napoleon Green had been acting very strangely the night before the tragedy and openly boasted to his room mates; "Ah intend to mow down a few of you's guys tomorrow, especially that bastard Ader." He was referring to Captain Ader, the Provost Marshal, who was due to interview Green later that day on charges of theft and indecently assaulting a young girl. In his outburst that night, Green added; "Now, you listen to me you's guys, tomorrow I die but I shall come to the mess hall at twelve o'clock and rub you all out." However, his rantings and threats were not taken seriously and nobody reported the affair to a senior officer.

Before he went off to work with Leon Thorn, the airport gardener on that fateful morning, Green left a hastily scribbled note on his locker. It read; "Today, I die". After leaving the hut, Green commenced work with Leo Thorn trimming the lawn edge surrounding the Officers Mess. A few minutes later, Green darted away to the base armoury and forced the master sergeant to hand over a .30 calibre carbine and a .45 revolver. Threatening the senior N.C.O. with violence he grabbed the weapons and snatched up a handful of ammunition. Frenziedly, the crazed black man loaded both firearms and grabbed more ammunition, some contained in magazines. Then holding the carbine close to his hip, and the revolver in the other hand, he ran out of the armoury and headed for the huts. Kicking open the door of Hut 848, Green yelled to the off duty airmen - "Get out of here by ten o'clock or else, you bastards." The utterly bewildered occupants simply stared at his rapidly disappearing figure as he rushed past Leo Thorn, leaving him reeling in surprise.

Just then Airman Second Class Nelson Gresham dashed over to Green and pleaded with him as a fellow black man to drop the weapons before anyone got hurt. Napoleon responded with a burst of fire from the automatic at point blank range and the courageous Greshsam was dead before hitting the ground. Sergeant

Above: Napoleon Green

Left: Miss Wendy Walton

Hugh Parker who had seen what was going on made a gallant attempt to impede Green, but was stopped in his tracks by a single bullet. Fortunately, his injuries were slight but enough to prevent him from pursuing the deranged airman who was now running in circles and obviously out of his mind. Green fired at anyone who ventured too near, directing savage bursts of fire at Sergeant Gouvier and Airman Lester Hunt. Luckily, they were only slightly wounded.

Green then sprinted into the pay office, where without the slightest warning or provocation, he shot Sergeant Lawrence Velasquez, a father of four, dead. Wendy Walton, a junior pay clerk, watched in utter disbelief as the sergeant slid to the floor in a pool of blood. Screaming hysterically, she rushed to the door but never made it as Green shot her in the thigh. Later she was treated successfully at Ramsgate Hospital. After shooting Wendy, Green gripped the seemingly paralysed Shirley Hall by the arm in an attempt to drag her away. R.A.F. Corporal Grayer who was unofficially engaged to her, dashed forward and commanded Green to take his hand off the girl. But the American simply pointed the revolver at him and pulled the trigger. Corporal Grayer died shortly afterwards. A civilian employee, Audrey Easto, who had been slightly injured in the first volley of shooting said at the inquest; "I don't think Corporal Grayer would have died if he had kept quiet."

On leaving the pay office, Green ran towards the main entrance and before reaching the gate, stopped an incoming van at gunpoint. The astonished driver, Leonard Broadbent of Margate, had four passengers and all they could do was

American Servicemen act as stretcher-bearers to carry Green from the beach to the waiting Ambulance after the final dramatic battle. This picture was taken by Mrs. Hodgkinson

gaze in horror and in disbelief as Green pointed the carbine at the side of the van and nonchalantly sprayed the vehicle from bonnet to boot with a hail of bullets. Miraculously, not one of them was killed. As Green ordered them out of the van, Ian Yeomans of Ramsgate was shot in the buttocks but managed to scramble out followed by Ann Cockburn of Broadstairs who had been shot in the leg. The other two passengers both females, were unhurt. Green, realising that this shooting of the van had rendered the vehicle useless, loped off to the main gate, where he found the unsuspecting Sergeant Rolly McDaniels sitting in his car. After firing a short burst at an incoming car, Green pointed the revolver at the head of McDaniels. "Ah'm not afraid of you mister" Green snarled; "You just do as you are told and drive like hell you hear man?" As the sergeant said later at the inquest; "I just drove like he said" explaining that Green was pointing a gun at his head he felt he didn't have a choice. Continuing his narrative he said; "When we reached a crossroads just outside Margate, he said he wanted to go to London. I told him I was low on gas, which was true. By then I had started talking to this madman and I suggested that he might like to drive himself. This I thought, would allow me to contact the Police. To my surprise, he agreed and after I had shown him the controls, I got out and ran like hell. I hitched a lift from a passing motorist and went straight to the police station. When I left the car, Green shouted out; "Tell that bastard Captain Ader that when they get me boy, ah will be dead". As Green drove off alone, the police had already been alerted and given a description of McDaniels car and registration number, so road blocks were instantly set up. Constable Bert Bridgeland who lived a few yards from the crossroads, saw

McDaniels running frantically past his house as he was getting ready for motor cycle patrol duty. A witness gave him a brief description of the car and Bert set off in pursuit after pausing to don his uniform and motor cycle boots. By the time he set off, Green was about to enter the sleepy little town of Broadstairs.

Driving at breakneck speed down Harbour Street, he left the car parked right outside the Tartar Frigate public house which faces the harbour. The time then was 10.45 a.m. and Green had no idea that at least 16 police officers, some armed, and a strong posse of U.S.A.F. military police had been following him. Seventy year old Fred Beecham the harbour car park attendant, was very annoyed when he saw Green leave the car parked in Harbour Street, instead of in his car park. Angrily, the old chap shouted as he hobbled over to the steps leading to the beach down which Green had fled. He called out; "Hey mister you can't park there, you're obstructing the road". His tone may have been different if he realised the man he was slating, had just slaughtered three men in as many minutes. Green turned round to face Fred Beecham as he ran off towards North Foreland stumbling on the seaweed covered rocks. He shouted to Fred Beecham; "You tell them old man, that if they want me, they'll have to come and get me." Fred Beecham was still seething when he was brushed aside by Green's pursuers. They could now see their quarry as he scrambled over the slippery rocks at the foot of the 60ft. high cliffs.

Green was still clutching the firearms and hundreds of holiday makers were thoroughly entertained by the chase and the exchange of shots between Green and his hunters. Those who glanced up at the promenade would have seen a back up squad of armed American police keeping up with the chase and firing at the fleeing negro. As it was their attendance was not required as shortly afterwards the drama terminated. By then the American had covered more than a mile of the foreshore, occasionally turning to fire at his pursuers. At a point not far from the steps leading to a house on the promenade once owned by a prominent Nazi, Green suddenly stopped and in slow motion turned the barrel of the automatic against his chest. One shot was enough, it was all over leaving the bewildered onlookers to speculate as to what ignoble impulse had made this foreign ally run amok.

A Foul Murder in Room 66

In the afternoon of October 23rd 1929, handsome, debonair Sydney Harry Fox, thirty years old and unemployed, booked in at the luxurious Metropole Hotel, overlooking Margate Harbour, accompanied by his 63 year old mother - Rosalind Fox, the widow of a railway signalman. Her sole income was five shillings a week pension. Before arriving at Margate, the pair stayed at the County Hotel, Canterbury, the Royal Pavilion Hotel, Folkestone, the Savoy also in Folkestone and the Grand Hotel at Dover. They stayed in only the best hotels but invariably departed without paying the bill. At the opulent Grand Hotel in Dover, they left with alacrity and indeed furtiveness, in the early hours, leaving their account of £3, 5 shillings unpaid. Wherever they stayed, only a small amount of luggage accompanied them, but evidently this was not viewed with suspicion by the managements concerned.

Before coming to Kent, probably from London or Norwich, their home town, Sydney Fox, a very plausible fraudster, thief and later murderer, went to great lengths to ensure that his mother's life was adequately insured and the first policy was taken out in March 1929, probably for six months as it expired at midnight on 23rd October that same year. Fox made sure that he paid Cornhill Assurance Company the premium of twenty five shillings and sixpence. For some undisclosed reason, he also paid in an additional twelve shillings and sixpence. In any case, he was quite satisfied that the life of his mother was fully covered in the sum of three thousand pounds, as long as she died before midnight on the day of their arrival in Margate; otherwise, the policy would be utterly useless. Sixty years ago, three thousand pounds was a sizeable fortune, enough to purchase several houses at least. However, it seems that this sum was not enough for the nefarious Sydney, one of the very few men found guilty of matricide in this country. He tried to insure his mother's life with the Sun Assurance for one thousand pounds, and also with the Royal Assurance Company for the sum of two thousand pounds. Both companies promptly rejected his proposal forms allegedly signed by Mrs Fox.

Undeterred but very annoyed, Sydney Fox decided to take out a policy on the life of his current girlfriend, the extremely wealthy Australian born Mrs Morse, who was living apart from her husband who remained in Australia. Now, this foolish woman had no knowledge of this insurance policy, neither was she aware that Fox had forged her signature on the proposal form, as he had done with his mother's insurance proposal form. We can safely assume that if Mrs Morse had known of her lover's intentions, she would have promptly returned to the Antipodes. For Sydney Fox, womaniser and con man extraordinary, had captivated her to such an extent that she altered her will and made him the sole beneficiary. She was also imprudent enough to tell him this but she was not to know that the only income of Fox was an Army Invalidity Pension of eight shillings a week and even this had been obtained by deception.

His life of crime began even before leaving school at the age of thirteen, when he was birched for stealing. I find it rather strange that his criminal background never came to the notice of the London bank manager who took him on as a junior clerk in 1915. Perhaps the War and the calling up of thousands of young men, seriously thinned the ranks of aspiring bank employees. As a rule, banks made careful enquiries into the antecedent history of their employees. His stay at this particular bank was purely transient, and he was dismissed on the spot when it was discovered he was stealing and forging cheques. Oddly enough there seems to be no record of Fox ever being prosecuted for this. At the age of 17, with the war in full swing, he joined the Royal Army Ordnance Corps; again, it appears that he was accepted without details of his criminal past coming to light. Private Fox obviously found life in the R.A.O.C. rather tedious as he very soon applied for a transfer to the newly formed Royal Air Force. Surprisingly, his request was granted without delay.

Having settled down in the R.A.F., Fox reverted to his old habits of stealing and forging cheque books. He was probably an officer's batman, I cannot possibly imagine him holding a commissioned rank, and as a batman he would be in an ideal situation to indulge in such activities.

When he was eventually arrested in a West End night club, this young rake was wearing the uniform of an Army Lieutenant - this would be an offence in itself - and he was sent to prison for eight months. On his release, this incorrigible and plausible rogue even managed to wangle his way back into the Army, where he remained until July 1929. Naturally, he made sure that he was never sent to France and of course saw no action. In early 1929, he applied for a discharge on medical grounds and asked to be considered for the award of an invalidity pension. He repeatedly reported sick, claiming that he suffered from epilepsy and gave excellent exhibitions of epileptic symptoms which he claimed were caused by his Army service. He eventually convinced an unusually gullible Medical Board and was discharged with a pension of eight shillings weekly.

And so we come to the night of 23rd October 1929, when at ten p.m. Mrs Fox retired to bed in Room 66. As usual, Sydney entered her room to kiss her goodnight but instead, he ruthlessly strangled the old woman as she sat in an armchair. Later the time of death was reckoned to be 10.40. At his trial held at Lewes Assizes, the Attorney General was prompted to remark to the jury in his summing up speech, - "What were the thoughs of this evil man as he ascended the hotel stairs and then entered his mother's room?" Just before he went upstairs, Fox showed his appreciation of the music provided by Reg Crouch and his band by buying drinks all round. "Put it on my bill" he told the barman.

After strangling his mother, he placed her body on her bed and lit a fire under her chair near the bed hoping no doubt that when the horse hair in the chair

The Metropole Hotel in the centre of Margate

ignited, the smoke emitted would be sufficient to convince a doctor that she had died from suffocation through inhalation of the smoke as she lay in bed. In fact, that was the diagnosis put forward by the first doctor on the scene - Dr Austen, when he attended and examined the body. Fox told the Police and the firemen that he was awakened by the smell of thick and acrid black smoke which billowed into his adjoining room through the connecting door which was closed. "The smoke was so dense" said he, "that I found it impossible to get into my mother's room, although I tried very hard to do so." Dr Nicol who also attended, concurred that Mrs Fox had died from asphyxia caused by the inhalation of smoke. However, at the trial, both practitioners changed their minds about the cause of death, but only after hearing the unshakeable evidence of that legendary Home Office pathologist, Dr Bernard Spilsbury, who conducted the post mortem examination. This was done at the request of Superintendent Ayto of New Scotland Yard and Detective Sergeant Hambrook. They had been alerted by Inspector Palmer of Margate Police and on 11th November, 1929, the body which was interred at Great Frensham Norfolk, was exhumed.

They were fully justified in taking that step after hearing what the Cornhill Assurance employees had to say. There is no doubt that suspicion would not have focussed quite so swiftly on to Fox, had he curbed his insatiable greed and restrained his impatience to get hold of the insurance money. By repeatedly asking the Assurance company for an advance, he ensured their suspicions would be aroused, as indeed they were. The Scotland Yard detectives became even more suspicious when they received full details of the antecedent history of Fox, which included the fact that he was an undischarged bankrupt. Fox made it even worse for himself by informing the Assurance Company that he was the sole beneficiary in his mother's will, before she was buried. Sydney Fox was very angry and disappointed when he was told of the unavoidable delay in settling the claim and he had the temerity to approach one of the senior partners of a well known and long established firm of solicitors Girling and Wilson. He spun such a convincing tale to Mr A E. Wilson that the gullible lawyer handed over two sums of money amounting to £40; this was on 29th October, 1929 six days after killing his mother.

Following the examination and the damning evidence of Dr Spilsbury, Fox was charged with the murder of his mother, obtaining credit by fraud without disclosing that he was an undischarged bankrupt. The lengthy trial, which attracted large numbers of the opposite sex, at Lewes Assizes, began during the first week of March, 1930. Fox pleaded not guilty and continued to proclaim his innocence throughout his trial. The evidence of Dr Spilsbury was without doubt the most valuable for without it, there would have been no murder trial. Defending Counsels Mr Cassells and Mr James, tried hard to convince Mr Justice Rowlett and his jury that Mrs Fox died of asphyxia through inhalation of smoke and during the proceedings, a small quantity of horsehair was ignited in Court to demonstrate just how quickly a dense cloud of smoke could be ignited. The chair too was produced as an exhibit.

Mr Cassels and his partner must have known that they stood no chance of disproving the evidence by this colossus of the pathological world, especially when two of their witnesses, the local doctors, suddenly changed their diagnosis to concur with that given by Spilsbury. This eminent man was quite convincing when he explained that he found bruising on the neck of Mrs Fox, together with bruising on her tongue and on her thyroid cartilage. A portion of this cartilage preserved in glycerine was produced but predictably, it was not examined by the Counsel for the Defence. Nothing could shake or discredit the evidence of Dr Spilsbury, who was certain beyond any doubt that Mrs Fox had been strangled before the fire was started in her room.

As each of the twenty witnesses testified, the evidence against Fox became even more overwhelming and yet right through his nine day trial, he vehemently maintained that he did not kill his mother. "Yes," he said, "I am an undischarged bankrupt and I forged and stole cheques and I could not pay the hotel bill; but I did not murder my mother." One of his brothers stated that the handwriting on the insurance proposal form was not that of his mother, but that of his brother Sydney. He also included the fact that his mother's will was written by his brother Sydney.

Counsel for the Prosecution - the Attorney General Sir William Jewett and Sir Henry Curtis, placed great importance on the inescapable fact that Mrs Fox died before midnight on 23rd October 1929 and her insurance cover expired precisely at that time and on that day.

Sydney Harry Fox

When the Attorney General made his final speech in his summing up, he declared that the fact that the murdered woman was the mother of Fox, rendered the case unparalleled in legal history and his actions were incredibly callous. Fox was of course sentenced to death by hanging and he was the last man to be executed at Maidstone on 8th April, 1930, and in addition to joining the ranks of those odious few who have committed matricide, he also became the only condemned man to have divorce papers served on him a few hours before he died, which named him as co-respondent. Mr Morse had no qualms about initiating this course of action. Later that year, Fox was rated as sufficiently notorious to justify his effigy being placed in Madame Tussauds. So ended one of the most bizarre murders in the history of Kent.